Elephant on the Chips

Elephant on the Chips

Lessons of Leadership from Life

Paddy Rao

PARTRIDGE
A Penguin Random House Company

To order additional copies of this book, contact
Partridge India
000 800 10062 62
www.partridgepublishing.com/india
orders.india@partridgepublishing.com

CONTENTS

In memory of my father, of whom I have no memory.

PREFACE

The nor'easter was doing what it does best in Boston, dumping fourteen inches of snow and whistling its way back, as if it was challenging the tenacity of Bostonians. We were tired of the deep winter that year and were in no mood to face up the nor'easter, and so the entire city shut down. We just decided to stay indoors, not to shovel the snow from the driveway, but sit back, relax, and watch the snow pile up. And watch TV.

The cable network was full of news anchors and weather persons competing with each other to bring us the latest snow update. Being competitive was the core definition of being an American, and it showed.

Indian TV channels flashed on the large screen as I got bored with the weather updates about Boston and started flipping through them aimlessly. Suddenly something caught my attention. What, an elephant roaring in the busy marketplace of Delhi? While it was common for American and European TV channels to always associate elephants, tigers, and snakes with India, why was the Indian TV channel showing an elephant on the busy streets of Delhi? That too in the bedlam of Chandni Chowk market?

The Indian TV channel news anchor was taking the listeners through a short history of the busy Chandni Chowk market.

'Do you know who designed and built this market?' she was asking no one particular. Without waiting for any response, she took upon herself the burden of educating the viewers. 'This was built by Mughal Emperor Shah Jahan in seventeenth century to the design of his daughter Jahan Ara,' she said as if it mattered so much to the scene that was unfolding. Why do TV producers go all over while telling a story? They seem to be in awful pressure to fill the time somehow.

I got very impatient to know what the elephants were doing in such a busy market that was infamous for selling counterfeit brands. The news anchor did what they are very good at—interrupting interesting news with some boring commercials.

I was compelled to watch an obese kid drooling over his mom's delicious food and a couple of daughters-in-law glaring at their mother-in-law and tolerate Intel boasting how it was inside everything.

The commercials over, the news anchor smiled again. 'The US Government has been leaning on India to act sternly and swiftly to protect the Intellectual Property rights.' The newsreader continued, 'So to demonstrate its commitment, our government is having a show of counterfeit products being crushed by elephants. Seeing this visible demonstration, it is hoped that people will stop buying or selling counterfeit products.' She gave a quick sideways glance to check if the appropriate video footage was ready to be beamed.

A truck pulled in and dumped loads of counterfeit software, CDs, DVDs, IC chips, and Ray-Ban products. At a signal from a police officer, skinny guys who were commandeering the large elephants whispered something in their ears, and the elephants trampled on the counterfeit goods and crushed them to powder. The whole crowd went delirious, and everyone laughed.

I laughed too but soon fell thinking, looking back at my Bangalore-Boston marathon, at my exciting life journey over the last fifty years.

I had never thought I would end up in Boston, but here I was. The Bangalore-Boston life marathon took nearly fifty years to do, as I went to different parts of the world and even circumnavigated the world like Magellan.

This journey morphed me from being a newly-wed spouse whose only earthly possession was a cotton blanket and a folding chair into a middle-aged spouse who could gift his wife diamond jewellery at will. Not bad at all!

Like Tom Hanks in the movie *Forrest Gump*, I was lucky to be in the right places to meet global business leaders like Jeff Immelt, Azim Premji, Narayana Murthy; correspond with George Sudarshan trying to prove Einstein wrong (what was I thinking?); walk the infinite corridors of MIT in Boston; give a speech in the Mary Gates hall in Seattle; and meet with great yogis trying to understand the secret of who we are. Chance sighting of maestros like Sunny Gavaskar, Ilayaraja, Kamal Hasan, and the Dalai Lama would help me learn lessons through mere observations of how they dealt with their celebrity status and behaved in public.

Why did the video clip of an elephant on the chips trigger me to think of my life journey? Was it because the journey was as surreal as the scenario that unfolded on TV? Or was it because my response to challenges I faced was as unorthodox as the elephant trampling the chips? Or was the elephant a metaphor for common men and women who can crush the life's challenges at will? I had no idea but continued to think nevertheless.

What struck me as more important at the end of this reminiscing was the recognition that anyone could surmount all odds and come out as successful as me if they tried hard enough. Life does not pick winners and losers, *but we make ourselves winners or losers.*

It felt as if everything we needed to know was hidden in our brain for us to discover. We all have a Magellan hiding in ourselves, willing to cross the seven seas of self-doubt, fatalism, resignation, bad luck, blaming others, hurdles, and the unknowns in a daring quest for success in life. We are never alone in this journey. We do get help and support from those who love and respect us.

Two women helped shape me up and chase my destiny. First, my mother, Saraswathi—an uneducated, orthodox poor young widow of thirty who never remarried—pulled me ashore by her sheer grit, discipline, and sacrifice. The other is an angel spouse, Jayanthi, who is far more talented and made of better moral fibre than me, who tamed the wild horse in me, guided me, and paid the price for my failings.

I owe my life to my mother, and all success to my wife.

This is the core of the story Elephant on the Chips—personal leadership builds character and gives courage and guts to face any odds to come out winning. *And this is learnt from our life*, not *from a fancy management school.*

This is not about the life story of a privileged or a genius kid. This is the story of a typical man or woman in the world; mind you, no one in the world is average unless one decides to be. All are born with same faculties, and the only difference is in the environment we all face. Everyone has the same opportunity to face and overcome the obstacles the environment throws at them.

People become what they let themselves be. The key to success is learning early on that our imitations are a product of our thinking and hence we have the ability to break free. Dhirubhai Ambani, the legendary founder of Reliance Industries, was a son of a poor schoolteacher and he worked as a gas station attendant in Aden, Yemen, during his teens. He died the second-richest man in the world, building the biggest private enterprise in India. How did he do it?

As I looked back, I was amazed at the way things shaped up in my life. My life moved as though it was influenced by principles that were paradoxical in nature. They were paradoxical not because they were, but because we did not expect that they would turn out that way. If we understand that, we are in command of twists and turns; if not, we get surprised at every turn, and we go on blaming some unseen fate.

What were the paradox principles that I learnt from my life?

1. Lead yourself, if you want to lead others.
2. If you are in a hurry, slow down.
3. To get something, give up what you have.
4. To win, let others win.
5. To win, prepare to lose.
6. To be there, be here.
7. To be admired, create a conflict.
8. To learn everything, unlearn yourself.

There is a new 'spice route' waiting to be discovered by everyone in the world for themselves, and so is a Magellan hiding in everyone . This book is an effort to help every reader unwrap their Magellan, learn from their respective lives, and discover new ways.

Come, let us hear my Magellan's story.

TO LEAD OTHERS,
LEARN TO LEAD YOURSELF.

CHAPTER 1

⌘

Being Everything without Being Anything

'He must be sleeping,' said a young boy as he peeped in through the window of the Ambassador car. We were seated in the front row of the car, with my dead father lying cold at the back. We were waiting for our sister to be fetched from her school.

'No, he must be dead,' commented his friend.

The taxicab driver was very proud that his car could hold four kids, two adults, and a dead body. He commented aloud that it was the smallest big car while being biggest small car at the same time. That remark was definitely out of place but still made much sense. We could hardly fault the taxi driver for not associating with and sharing our grief.

I was about eight years old and was sitting on the lap of my grandfather in the front seat of the taxi. He had come to fetch us back to Chennai as soon as he got to hear of my father's sudden death. My father was only thirty-nine years old when he died.

My elementary schooling in this salubrious, plateau city of Bangalore was over.

I had thoroughly enjoyed the schooling there and did not want to leave. We were living in a remote development at the south end of Bangalore. The development had a few houses, a common well, and a big rumour that foxes visited the place in the night-time. Some with vivid imagination, and an even stronger sense of hearing, talked of visitations by a lonely tiger. We kids hoped desperately that some day we would get a glimpse of the tiger, but it never happened. The foxes and tigers stayed safe in the rumour mills.

The folks who lived there were simple-minded, and if we went by their festivals, even ghosts were simple-minded. They celebrated the love god festival every year in springtime. Ghosts were rumoured to be sneaking in the night to steal firewood and cow dung cakes. So, what did the simple villagers do? They just wrote on their doors 'Come tomorrow' so that ghosts could read that and just go away. The ghosts did exactly as expected, and this continued till the ghosts got tired and stopped coming.

Bangalore sits on a plateau about 3,000 feet high, making it a pleasant place; it rained almost every day in the afternoon. It had so many lakes and gardens and we were all proud to call it Kent of India, although none of us had ever seen *the* Kent of England.

On weekends, we kids played the pin-down game on the muddy playground. It was played with a rusted iron pin thrown forcefully on the mud; if it stood, you won, and if it fell down, you lost. Once I got so worked up during the game, I kept throwing the pin till I missed and it pierced my brother's toe. He bled a bit but covered it up from my parents. They were disciplinarians and most probably would have punished me hard.

My elementary school was a strange one. It was a small private school called Vyas Bala Mandir, in which students from many levels were bunched in same classroom. You could see K1 to K3 (or grade 1 to grade 3) bunched together in one classroom with the same teacher handling all the subjects. It meant you had unofficial breaks when your friend was being taught while you simply watched—you were from a different class and hence were not required to be attentive.

This gave us an opportunity to 'up learn' higher-class lessons even when we were struggling in our lower-level lessons! The best part I liked was that on many days I got the duty of ringing the school bell. It was a kind of big hand bell that you had to hold with both hands to ring. I was ringing the bell in so many different ways and so well that very soon many teachers declared I was very intelligent. It sure rang a bell in our Shyamala teacher. She encouraged me to be different and hoped that I would be a famous scientist one day. I took her advice seriously and began my own experimentation at home. I collected turmeric, vermillion, and other powders, mixed them with water, and made colourful liquids and filled them in small bottles. I would collect my sister's classmates and explain the liquids using all sorts of science-sounding words and they would be wide eyed and impressed. I felt great, like Pierre Curie.

My two elder brothers went to St Joesph's High School, a missionary school a few miles away, at Bryant Square. Unlike my Vyas Bala Mandir, it was a reputed school and part of the great global institution of Society of Jesus. Yes, the same one St Ignatius Loyola started in 1540 in Europe under the approval of Pope Paul III.

The senior leadership of these institutions were Jesuits, or 'God's marines', who devoted their life for the uplift of human life through right education. They came early on to India with one of the founders, Father Xavier, reaching Goa as early as 1541. The Jesuits were well received and honoured in Akbar the Great's court.

No Vyas Bala Mandir this!

The Jesuit who taught at their school would occasionally come to our neighbourhood to see my brothers and his friends. I would run along to see him and listen to whatever they were talking about. Somehow, I wanted to be them rather than what I was.

This urge to be somebody else would continue throughout my life. Much later in life, I learnt that wanting to be somebody else is a positive frustration that can be the genesis of a *drive* to improve or pursue some great things. While many argue that we have to learn to be comfortable in our skin, nature may be finding its way towards evolution by driving small kids to daydream and want to be somebody else.

I went daydreaming with gusto: yesterday I was a scientist, today a cricketer, and tomorrow an adventurer. As I kept meeting adults from different fields, I wanted to be all of them, sometimes Individually and sometimes all rolled in to one—any combination that would impress people.

My school, Vyas Bala Mandir, was one day shut down, and I moved to St Joseph's High school. I was not sure why the school was shuttered. Maybe the all-in-one classroom was not fancied by many parents. While I was happy to move on to a bigger and better school, I did miss the strange classes and the bell-ringing job.

While it felt great that I was now going to one of the best schools in Bangalore, it was intimidating too. The classes were truly independent, and the teachers spoke and taught in good English. Many of the non-Jesuit teachers were 'Anglo-Indian', which was a mixed race, a consequence of British rule in India during which some of the British cohabited with Indians. Most of the Anglo-Indians emigrated to United Kingdom, Australia, and Canada once the British granted independence to India and left in 1947.

The Anglo-Indian teachers spoke with a British accent, which I simply could not follow. This led to a comedy of errors when one of them gave me a rotten apple to throw and I politely kept declining to accept the gift. She burst into laughter and tried to explain that she wanted me to just throw it away!

All that daydreaming was suddenly cut short one afternoon, when my father's friend came to fetch me. He mumbled something to my class teacher, and she looked pathetically at me. What was that? She would not say anything except telling me that I should not lose heart and I had much of life ahead of me. I simply did not get it.

What was that again? My father's friend would not say anything either. We walked silently through the long corridors that led us into a big playground. We went past the ground and got straight into one of busiest streets of Bangalore. City Market was a sheer madness of hundreds of people, shopkeepers, hawkers, auto-rickshaws, and bicycles, all fighting for the same single lane of a narrow road.

We crossed the world-famous Tipu Sultan fort, and I very badly wanted to check if the crocodiles were up for lunch in the moat as the rumour mill always mentioned. My father's friend literally had to drag me into the Victoria Hospital as I was looking around, fascinated by the maddening crowd. The hospital was a very beautiful building, built by the British to commemorate the reign of Queen Victoria.

As we got into the sombre hospital, he was lying there motionless, and dead, with his hands folded like he was praying. He died in a rush at the ripe age of thirty-nine. He had left behind four small children; I was the third child and eight years old. He was reportedly feeling uncomfortable a few days back and had got himself admitted in the hospital, just for a check-up. He was an officer in the Federal Reserve Bank of India and felt responsible enough to work on his deathbed. All of a sudden his heart gave away, just like that!

My brothers were crying, my mom was crying, and so were my father's friends. I walked out into the corridor and sat down on a bench stoically and did not cry.

We were sitting in the taxi, waiting for my sister to get back from her school. She came in soon enough, and promptly started wailing. Due to some strange reason, I did not cry. Everyone pleaded that I cry and let it out, but I would not. Maybe I could not visualise the consequence, future, or anything else in detail; maybe I kind of dissociated myself from the whole situation and perhaps behaved a bit badly.

We all got into the car and started our journey some 200 miles east to the port city of Chennai. My grandfather, a retired high school headmaster, lived there, and we were seeking refuge in him. The drive took several hours, and the presence of my father's dead body in the car made the journey longer and unbearable. I sat in the front and kept gazing at the front window of the car and never looked back. My mother was naturally distraught and tried hard to keep her composure. All of us were preparing ourselves for a future that looked so uncertain.

We reached my grandfather's home in Chennai late at night, and the whole street was waiting for us. The neighbours were shocked that one of their friends had died at a young age of thirty-nine. Over the next few days, we went through the heart-rending last rites; scores of relatives kept coming to express their grief a sympathies. They were very sorry to see a young widow and small children who now faced uncertainty.

To be honest, it felt truly good with all the sympathy flowing towards us. Our family friends, acquaintances, and even those we had met by chance would enquire about us and express shock and sympathy on hearing our story. This continued for several months to the extent that we always anticipated that someone would ask, and we were ready with our story; the appendage of 'poor children' always felt good. This went on for too long, and one of our relatives helped break that shell and let us free from this cage of self-pity.

He was a high school teacher, and like all high school teachers in India, he was poor in money but enormously rich in kindness. He sternly told us, 'You kids have no one to guide or help. You are getting drowned in a flood of good-intentioned sympathy. This may make you feel wonderful for some time but is very harmful for your future. You will get trapped in this self-pity, which is not an alternative to self-esteem. There is no one to pull you out of this trap, and so how would you do that?' We kids had no idea what he was talking about and kept silent.

'Very simple,' he continued. 'Either you sacrifice all the fun and merrymaking for the next ten to fifteen years, focus on studying, get good college degrees that will fetch you a good paying job, and you can relax and enjoy for the rest of your lives. The alternative is to drown in the wave of sympathy and self-pity, spending years playing and enjoying like other kids do. This would perhaps risk losing focus and you will fail in education and suffer for life. Remember, other kids have a father as a safety net and you don't. Revelling in sympathy will set you back forever.'

I never ever forgot that advice; it travelled with me for the next fifteen years, as I kept meeting friends of varying background. Often I would get tempted to relax and lower guard, and every time I would remind myself of the caution that uncle gave and stay focused on my studies. I picked my friends carefully, with no partying and no clubbing, as we could afford none of that. The only thing we could afford to do was to learn to be creative as far as money and expenses were concerned.

For example, I became a Boy Scout before I formally became a Boy Scout.

My brother and I wanted to become Boy Scouts, but my mom could afford to sponsor only my brother, even though it only cost us a few more cents per month. We just had to be very careful with whatever insurance money our father had left us. But I would go with him to the scout grounds, sit about twenty feet away, crane my ears and eyes to catch some words as the scoutmaster would teach, and learn.

My scout guru was very pleased with my dedication and allowed me to join and learn anyway. We finally managed to find enough money for me to join the team. The scout programme was so timely and essential for us. It built character and self-reliance. It filled the gap left by our father's premature death.

As I became a Boy Scout formally, the scoutmaster introduced me to the programme. 'The entire Boy Scouts programme is designed to inculcate the movement's motto "Be prepared" in our minds,' he said. 'Prepared for what? As a scout, we have to pledge ourselves in the service of God, country, and ourselves. This cannot be truly accomplished unless we prepare ourselves to lead in the service, and this preparation is all about getting trained in several skills.

'We need to constantly to build ourselves and be self-reliant, be physically fit, and learn to camp, cook, first aid, and swim among other things. The basic premise is that you train to lead yourselves first before you build the capability to lead others. You learn different skills, qualify through tests, and start earning badges leading you to second class, first class, and beyond. You are ready to lead them,' he concluded.

This became the core value that drove the first twenty years of my life. *Learn to lead yourself first, before you want to lead others.*

This idea developed into something more significant philosophically as I started reading Socrates and ancient Indian thoughts of the Upanishads. Their idea that you need to gain control over your own belief system and your own emotions made perfect sense.

How you react to other's provocations would depend on how you treat yourself—on par with others or as superior to others.

In other words, you treat yourself as an outsider, as an object to be led and conquered. If you don't know how to deal with yourself appropriately, you just would not know how to deal with anyone else at all. As simple as that. If you cannot lead yourself into 'victory', there is no way you will succeed in leading others. All this understanding will come over several years of battling dealing the usual assumption we all make when we are young—that we are right and always invincible.

It is another matter that we need our young to think they are always right and invincible to make progress and for 'pushing' the envelope.

Our grandfather lived in a big two-storeyed house that was shared by grandparents, two of my father's brothers, their spouses, and now the five of us. They were kind to let us live in the house and did not ask for any money. My father's life insurance money was promptly put away in a bank CD. The interest was used to fund our clothing, while the capital was reserved for the marriage of our kid sister.

So it was left to us three brothers to study hard, stay focused, and try to get scholarships to pay for our college education. My immediate elder brother, whom we affectionately called Cheenu, was blazing bright. He was always winning prizes, awards, and scholarships for his academic achievements. He was a voracious reader and was an active member of the American library, run by the American consulate. The books and magazines he borrowed provided a bright picture of the American way, and he loved it.

He would share very interesting stories of how Americans succeeded building the most powerful nation in the world. By the time I entered my teens, I came to know enough about Carnegie, Rockefeller, Getty, and Sloan. I learnt of GM's arrogance in declaring the infamous 'What is good for GM is good for America' line and the dishonest offer of Henry Ford for customers to choose any colour as long as it was black.

These stories about America created a powerful urge to be a part of the American dream, an urge that lay dormant in me for long, finally leading me to America in about thirty years. But how does a penniless kid get to America, and where does he start? My uncle's rebuke was perhaps the trigger.

It all started on a washing stone, a large slab of granite block that was fixed on an elevated platform built of sand, mortar, and cement.

Way back in early seventies, in India, clothes were washed by dunking them in a bucket of water, laying them over a washing stone, rubbing a detergent soap bar, and beating the clothes on the stone. My brother was sitting on that washing stone, and describing all the exciting stories he had read in the *Fortune, Life, Time,* and other magazines. I was sitting down on the floor below, with mouth gaping and jaws dropping, as he kept explaining. My maternal uncle saw this and snapped at me sarcastically that I should stop listening and start doing some talking myself if I wanted to get somewhere. His reasoning was that you could not talk unless you did and learnt something significant.

It bit me hard and provoked me deeply, but I held myself. He was right, in a way. I had turned out to be a shy boy, always short for words, withdrawn and nervous. This was not a great combination of skills to go and achieve something. I resolved to work hard to overcome these deficiencies as an answer to my uncle's rebuke.

The American Government was running several outreach programmes to help poor countries. It had a schools aid programme to help hundreds of high schools. The programme had teachers from US schools come and inspect how the programmes were really working. The visiting teachers invariably had a talk session with students.

During one of the visits, we had an American teacher talk about nature and free will. She was trying to exhort us to strive hard to come up in life and convince us that we could achieve anything if we wanted to.

'Isn't the so-called nature a consequence of repeated happenstance?' she asked rhetorically. 'If it so, it should also mean that with repeated efforts, one could change one's nature. There is nothing like a nature or fate, and so just go and do it,' she declared to a loud round of applause. This made me feel better and more confident about the resolve to get to America. There was a wide-open world out there bursting with opportunities, as per my brother; it seemed accessible to me only if one could talk and communicate well. If I could not even express myself, why would any strange land even take me in? I was not sure if this was true, but I somehow believed it. And there I was, unable to speak coherently outside the comfortable environs of my friends.

'How do I get over my nervousness and be good at public speaking? How do I tell my uncle that he was wrong in judging me harshly?' I kept thinking and went through the customary denial phase. 'Maybe I am not bad at all in public speaking,' I began to think, and it felt very good. That it was exactly opposite would hit me like a rock when I ventured to test it out.

I was in sixth grade and decided plunge into the area of discomfort, sign up in the elocution club, and take part in a competition to test it.

It was a simple school without much money, and hence it did not offer any fancy support—frankly, no support at all. The teacher in charge of the club just announced a date and registered the participants. On the day of contest, he simply called out the names and sat impassively behind a large desk.

I registered and prepared. How? Read pages of random books aloud; I stood in front of a mirror and talked to myself. I tried to catch hold of my friends and lectured them endlessly. Predictably, I lost many friends in the process. Did these things help me become a competent speaker? I would have to find out on the day of competition.

That day started uneventfully with a series of dull and boring classes. I was all the time thinking about the elocution contest scheduled in the evening and could not concentrate on the lessons at all. The school-closing bell gonged as the evening rolled in, and it was time to face the audience. I walked into the contest room full of eager students. The moderator started calling in the contestants one by one. It all appeared to go well till my name was called out.

I was all enthusiasm and energy as I walked briskly to the top of the class. It all vanished as I turned around and saw hundred boys sitting in front of me and staring menacingly at me. I stood there and froze.

Everyone waited for me to start talking, which I could not. I stood there, frozen, unable to say word. I started to speak haltingly, giving some encouragement to the audience who almost gave up on me. I felt encouraged too, and continued to mumble and then stopped again. This time, the class began to laugh at me. Many were smirking derisively as if they beat me down. There were a couple of kind souls who wanted to cheer me up, and they threw in abundant glances of kindness and understanding. I just kept looking at them, ignoring everyone else who were laughing, vomited all the memorised words, finished the speech, and ran out of the classroom. I kept running till I reached my home—tired, defeated, but not crying.

The first attempt to lead myself to glory in public speaking failed miserably, and I was plain wrong about my ability. What should I do now? Just give up and merge with the silent majority? Accept that skills and success are not something to be acquired with hard work, but were a gift of god? One has to be chosen one to be born with gift of the gab? Was the American teacher completely wrong when she told us that we could become anything we wanted to, if only we set our mind and worked hard?

'No way,' I thought. 'I will struggle, keep trying, and make it.' I would practise all the time, talking endlessly to my friends in lunch breaks. I then took it to next level and started talking to strangers in movie halls, restaurants, and other public places. The idea was to lose the idea of strangers and strangeness as they were obviously making me very nervous. I wanted to build an invisible bubble around myself, which was transparent on one side and opaque on the other.

Others could see me, but I won't be seeing them. I thought, 'If they don't exist in my view, how could they make me nervous?'

This worked and worked very well. I started gaining confidence in fluently addressing larger audiences; I competed again in elocution contests, and I gradually started winning. This kept going for a few years till I reached my high school graduation time and ended abruptly in a hilarious way.

It was a prestigious inter-school competition with nearly forty schools from the city competing. The format was elocution contest, which meant the topic was to be announced about a week ahead of the day of competition and all the contestants prepared and delivered their speeches. Forty of us were expected to prepare and deliver our version of what that topic meant for us, in full fifteen minutes.

A panel of four judges would decide who won; it was as simple as that. The four poor judges were to be subjected to the painful ordeal of listening to forty high school boys and girls waxing eloquent on the same topic. They still had to retain the sanity to be able to discern the difference and judge the winner!

The topic was announced: Character is the glory of life. How do you prepare for a topic like that?

My grandfather had taught English and math. He had even authored a textbook on high school math. In his library, he had a large leather-bound book full of well-written essays that not only impressed you but also moved the reader. They were written by old school English writers of nineteenth century in all flowery language and words. Fortuitously, that book had a great article with the same title, 'Character is the Glory of

Life'. The organisers seemed to have laid their hands on the very same book!

Somehow, I foolishly thought that perhaps only the two of us had that book, my grandfather and the elocution judge. This assumption would unravel on the day of competition.

It started well that day. We, the contestants, assembled in the school and were ushered into a large hall where we were treated to a sumptuous breakfast. After that, we moved into a large classroom, the venue of the contest, and took our seats.

One by one, the boys and girls were called upon to deliver their speeches. Every one called in before me delivered flowery oratory. As I kept listening to them, my heart pounded with excitement. I started wondering, 'What was the difference between oratory and elocution? Why was this competition called an elocution contest?' I did not know the difference and was curious to know at that very moment. But then, I needed to focus on the competition and win it, and so I pushed the curiosity away.

As I kept listening to the speeches, I started hearing Mark Antony in my mind, addressing the Roman public. I had read Shakespeare's *Antony and Cleopatra* drama, and as I sat there listening to other students, I could almost see Shakespeare smile at me emerging out of the book.

Why not talk like Mark Antony? His oratory was the cornerstone of the drama, a piece that has galvanised generations of orators and politicians. 'Yes, this will fetch me the prize,' I kept telling myself. I was getting very confident, comfortable, and almost smug.

The girl from the nearby school was announced next. She was cool, confident, poised and was not at all anxious or nervous. She almost floated on to the stage, stood, smiled, and started her speech. It sounded very good and was free flowing. Everyone was attentive and listening as she spoke in a measured way, with the right tempo and right pauses. She was simply brilliant, and it began to sink in me that we were looking at a potential winner.

I kept admiring her speech, and then I froze.

Every word she was saying was exactly the words that I was planning to say! How was that possible? Obviously, she also had the same book that had the collection of essays—not just me and the organisers!

What was I going to do? Should I say the same words, all of them, and become laughing stock of the room? Or quickly change the whole thing in my head and give a different speech? Was that even doable? I was scheduled to be the next speaker, and I just had a few minutes left before being called. The tension was so high that my brain almost stopped thinking. There was no way I could rewrite the entire speech in my head in the short time available, even if I wanted to.

What was I to do? The right thing to do would be not to surprise the judges by pretending to be different from her. I thought, 'Better take them into confidence and go by their call. If they permit, I would get to the stage and deliver my speech, modifying it as much as I could. If they asked me to leave, I would gladly do so.' This was my plan.

So, as the girl kept talking, I approached the organisers and told them of my predicament. They were not going to hear a different speech from me, and I offered to leave if they felt so. To my amazement, they said that it did not matter. It was elocution and not a debate contest. It all depended on how we delivered our speeches and not on the content.

The girl finished her speech, got a rousing appreciation, and everyone clapped. I was the next one to be called in. I walked on to the stage like a robot under master's command and started talking. Mark Antony descended on the stage and roared, 'Friends, teachers, and judges, lend me your ears,' and they obliged. This was a different start from anyone else's, so the audience got interested and listened. The difference died very soon and everyone started to hear the same words that the girl who spoke before me had delivered. It was as though someone had taped that girl's speech and was playing it back now. The boys and girls started breaking into smiles that soon became a crescendo of laughter. It was as if the girl's speech was coming back as an echo, except that it was being delivered in a male voice. It did not sound any better for that.

Everyone laughed, and the girl who was now sitting in the audience was not an exception. She simply could not control herself. It was one big laugh. But somehow it felt good to me too.

I finished my speech, and it was lunch break after that. I walked to the table where she was seated and said I was sorry. She regally asked why I was feeling sorry, half suppressing her smile. She did enjoy the speech, she said, and I believed her. After all, it was impossible for her to find out how her speech sounded and I solved it by doing her speech.

Somehow I felt at peace. I knew I had won, if not the trophy, my fear of public speaking was gone. Now

I could face any crowd and give any speech, without worrying about how they would receive it. It was very reassuring to know that we can overcome our perceived shortcomings with determination and persistent effort. It is entirely up to us to come up, and there is no point in blaming anyone or anything else for our failures.

This experience helped me recognise the power of humour in speeches as well. It was noticeable that while everyone kept laughing, no one wanted me to stop talking; they were completely connected with me. And that was the power of being funny on stage.

Oh, I never saw that girl again in my life!

This was the first learning in my life that *we need to learn to lead ourselves first, if we want to lead others.* Leading yourself means that you do not depend on others for guidance or support, but try to bootstrap yourself to victory. You set your goals, introspect to identify your weakness, and launch a self-improvement plan. Others can only provide a peripheral guidance as they cannot get into your heart or head to get a sense of what is driving you. You cannot let someone else light your fire; you have to do it yourself.

Leading yourself is harder than leading someone else, as you are battling yourself. The guy who wants to move forward and the guy who wants to stay behind are the same, and that is the biggest problem to solve. With sheer grit and perseverance, you can win this struggle. The biggest aiding factor in this is willingness to stand up every time you fall and somehow feeling that you will succeed next time. It can be irrational exuberance, but that is the antidote for the despondency.

The beauty of this learning is that it is universal and hence applicable to all; anyone who tries this will succeed. Success is guaranteed.

It was my dream to become an engineer, and this meant I had to do everything that would take me to that goal. No one else was going to do them for me. The requirement laid out by engineering colleges was that the aspiring students do a one year 'Pre-Degree PCM' course, studying physics, chemistry, and math.

There were many pre-degree colleges in Madras, but the Loyola College was considered to be the best for men. This was also a family tradition; my father studied there and so did my brother. The college was run by Society of Jesus and was famous for its discipline and academic brilliance. One had to score very high while graduating from high school to get admitted.

I worked hard and broke through what was known as '500 barrier'; only a tiny fraction of all students who appeared for the State Board final examination obtained 500 marks or more. I was very proud of myself with all friends and relatives fussing over me with awe.

It felt so very wonderful as many colleges invited me to join them. Almost all of them, except the Loyola College, sent in their admission notification very quickly. So, I waited to get the admit card from Loyola College, which I soon did. My pride increased, and I walked around with my chest all puffed up. I was now a 'Loyalite' as the students who went to Loyola College were called.

It seemed that I had defeated the challenge thrown at me by life; it snatched my father and financial well-being from me early in life, and I prevailed. 'Now I am going to the best college in the state,' I thought.

What a victory! This was a victory borne out of my first lesson—*lead yourself first, if you want to lead others*.

With this pride, I walked into the Loyola college, almost sure that I would get a hero's welcome.

On the very first day at Loyola College, my pride was crushed to a pulp.

IF YOU ARE IN A HURRY,
SLOW DOWN.

CHAPTER 2

—⋯—

Proving Einstein Wrong

It felt like being on the top of the world as I walked into the sprawling campus of Loyola College. It had all the ingredients of a great campus—spacious lawns, large European-style buildings, a great library, students' club, well-furnished dorms, and a beautiful church with a large steeple. With my chin up and puffing with pride, I entered the classroom.

The large classroom was filled with over sixty students from top high schools of country. We were all walking tall, me included. Why not? I was now a Loyolite, and it felt like we were from Yale or Harvard. 'Our next stop should be US Senate, as we cannot occupy the White House,' I thought.

It did not take long for me to realise that I was hardly the giant I imagined myself to be. The other students were not only brighter than me, but most of them seemed to be rich, sophisticated, and very Westernised. I just did not seem to belong there. It almost felt like being in a strange town. I just did not know how to push away my inferiority complex and merge into their world.

It was a steep climb indeed for me to try to be like them. The trouble was that I somehow felt it was necessary to be as good as they were to be a part of their group. It never occurred to me that it was not really necessary to be identical to belong. Every day was a struggle trying to look as good as them. It seemed to me that best way to be part of them was to beat them; but the more I tried to beat them, the more I felt I was falling behind. The more I tried to sound like them, the more I ended up looking like a poor imitation.

They talked of doing science projects on how earth's magnetic forces affected physical balances, and I did not know why. They discussed how chemicals combined to create magical compounds. This was too strange for me. They constantly talked about English fiction books, Hollywood movies, pop music, and the like; none of which made any sense to me at all. They were definitely in a different league.

I was tired of being at the bottom of the pile, poor, holding back on all the fun and frolic of life. I had worked so hard to get into the best college in south India, thinking that it will elevate my self-esteem, only to find that I felt myself to be at the bottom of the pile. It was becoming an obsession to get ahead to the top of the queue as soon as possible.

I was indeed in a hurry to do something big, be someone that every one admired and respected. I was willing to do anything, even outrageous stuff if needed, to get noticed. This is perhaps the normal human response, the common urge to break away from a position of disadvantage and succeed. But does it ever help feeling alienated and reaching to someone else on a rebound? I was going to learn the hard way.

While it was very difficult for me to break into that rich and elite crowd, I clearly saw that it was not their fault; they were all very nice and polite and made that extra effort to take me in. It was my feeling, my perceived inadequacy and the sense of not belonging there that came in the way. It was simply not possible to acquire their identity overnight, the one that they had painstaking cultivated over several years. I gave them a secret nickname, 'Yale group', in a mocking reference to the Ivy League College in America to which the rich and powerful sent their kids.

The next best thing I could do was to find a group that would be a comfortable fit for me. What might that group be? This was where I took a different tack. I thought, 'There must be other groups who felt as alienated with the "Yale" group, as I felt.' So instead of finding a group that shared my tastes, I kept looking for a group that shared my sad state.

Soon enough, I discovered a group that fitted like the proverbial glove. There were a few Jesuit brothers who were as alienated by the rest as I was. It was a bit strange too, as the institution was theirs, it belonged to their Society of Jesus, and these students were brothers, on their way to become Catholic priests.

It must have been very bizarre experience for them to be preparing to be Jesuits and yet be part of the mundane crowd like us, to be a part of the institution designed for them, and yet be alienated. They were also from another state, they spoke a different language from mine, and their English was halting. None of it seemed to matter, and we just bonded, brought together by the common feeling of alienation to the 'Yale group'. We held together for a year, and this 'belonging to the un-belonged' provided some degree of comfort. I pushed myself into hard work again, trying to graduate with flying colours to get into an engineering college.

During that period, I managed to complete a year's diploma in German language as well. Don't know why but it felt that every engineer in the world had to know German. After all, Germans made the best precision engineering, and how can you not speak their language and yet be an engineer?

There was another mental conflict brewing too—whether I should get into the prestigious IITs (Indian Institute of Technology) or a government-run engineering college. The IITs were established with enormous funding from the federal government and were on the same level as the Ivy league colleges of United States. It was not only very hard to get into any IIT, but also very expensive. While my family wanted me try to get into IIT, I made a firm decision that we simply could not afford it. Instead, I would apply for the state-run engineering college in Chennai that would practically waive all fees for me.

But then there was a difficulty waiting for me there too. The various governments had passed a quota law that reserved vast majority of seats to socially 'backward classes' to help the communities that were disadvantaged for centuries. In the long march of glorious history, India picked up a few blots in its character, and one such was the despicable caste system.

Over 4,000 years of evolution, Indian society had experimented with several ways to specialise in skills. The medieval Indians discovered that 'thinking skills' impacted larger number of people than 'muscle skills', 'trading skills', and 'service skills'. They started defining classes in society based on the skills people acquired and the trade they practised. Implicit in this classification was that those who chose the 'thinking' trade were superior.

For several centuries, this was a voluntary mechanism with anyone free to opt for any skill, work towards qualifying themselves, and gain respect. Slowly and steadily, this degenerated into a birthright-based caste system, taking an ominous turn, with generations getting condemned into 'lower skill' trades. Millions got suspended into this rigid system that denied any upward mobility based on choice and hard work. This oppressive caste system in India had pushed large sections to the bottom rung, and now it was their time to come up. Various governments had hence enacted laws establishing quotas for various downtrodden communities in every avenue of life. There were quotas in state-run colleges as there were quotas for jobs in state-run enterprises.

And here I was, a Brahmin, the most forward community, with no money but full of ambition and drive to come up in life. By the quota system, I had to do better than be in top 1 per cent to stand any chance in getting into the government colleges that waived tuition fee.

So it was back to the hard work regimen to get the best results possible in the exam, and sure I did get the best possible result. I passed out with a perfect score in math and distinction+ (95 per cent) in physics and chemistry. 'Maybe this is good enough,' we thought. There would be an interview too in the college selection process, but with this score, if I did very well in the interview, I was sure to get admitted. It all appeared to be wrapped up, until the result threw in a surprise.

The interview was a breeze, though a little bizarre. A panel of principals from five colleges interviewed a group of five students together. Of the five colleges, one was the government college in Madras and the others were either from some other city or private colleges, which meant they were out of my reach; either the tuition fee would be high, or I may have to pay for the dorm, which simply was out of question.

As the process rolled out, I felt very relieved and overjoyed; I answered not only all the questions addressed to me, but also the questions my group's fellow students could not answer. 'Boy wonder,' I thought of myself and whistled my way home and waited for results.

The results did arrive, and we were shocked to see that I was selected by the principal of PSG Engineering College in Coimbatore, a city couple of 100 miles away, and not by the government engineering college in Madras. This meant that I had to pay a hefty tuition and for the dorm. I had got myself admitted into something that we could not afford!

It seemed that the principal of PSG College was so impressed with my performance that he wanted me to join his college. His college was considered the best outside of IITs. However, there was no financial aid or tuition support, and hence none were offered. The reason to celebrate became the reason to feel sad.

With a heavy heart, I decided to drop the idea of becoming an engineer, collected myself, and joined the bachelor programme in Loyola College. 'If I cannot afford to be an engineer, I will become the next best thing, a physicist,' I thought.

My eldest brother, Viji, would not give up as easily I did. He had just then gotten married, and his father-in-law was a professor in Loyola College; he had a friend who was a professor in the government engineering college I was trying to get in. Perhaps he could put in a word explaining my situation to the principal and have my admission changed to the government-run college? He strongly felt it was worth a try.

We met him to explain that I had stellar credits but not so stellar a purse. It worked like magic, and my admission was changed to the government college in Madras.

I was whistling again till the college opened and I walked straight into groups of senior students. It was customary for the seniors to haze the freshmen students—it was called ragging—for a couple of weeks. The theory was that at the end of it, the seniors became good friends and helped with class notes. Stupidly, I believed every word of it and threw myself at the various groups of seniors. They had a field day in having fun at my expense for several days.

Much to my disappointment, not one of the seniors became my buddy ever, nor did I get one shred of class notes from them. It was torturous fun, though. I was a Napoleon giving a speech to troops on a moving bus one day, General Patton bullying the passengers in a subway train the other. I was herding a group of water buffaloes at the nearby dirty river or busy measuring the dimensions of a dorm room with a matchstick. The best I recall was me trying to demonstrate how to swim in a drop of water in the main foyer of the college with hundreds of boys and girls watching as they passed by. I participated in all these with gusto, and the word spread that there was this 'dope' (that was how freshmen were affectionately called by the seniors) who would do anything asked.

Finally, it was all over, and serious classes started. I loved physics and math, but chemistry and engineering drawing were horrors. I simply could not remember chemical names or why the O and H were arranged in a complex way in organic chemistry. The circles I drew with a compass always ended up as spirals. I could never successfully draw some strange shapes called cycloids, and my perspective lines never converged anywhere.

Much to my relief, we were informed that we would do away with all these things once we get into our third year of the five-year degree, if we got selected for Electronics. So I decided to become an electronics engineer!

But as I was in a hurry, I did not concentrate on what was in front of me—engineering drawing and chemistry. Instead, I was daydreaming about how I would get an honours degree in Electronics major. The cycloids and hydrocarbons nearly destroyed my chances, but I fought valiantly and vanquished them to get into Electronics major, eventually.

The engineering drawings and chemistry could not prevent me from having the typical college humour about the professors, though. Hurry or otherwise, humour cannot be taken out of college life.

Our favourite was the chemistry professor, who had a peculiar way of expressing himself. Like he once explained how 'the mercury get ups the tube' when we heat it with a Bunsen burner. Consider his friendly advice that we 'should stop rotating the hallways, go to the library, and expand our brains'. When he was upset that we were chatting and disturbing the class when he was busy teaching, he would yell that 'both the three of us' should get out of the class.

The English Professor Mr Praveen Issar was a different kind. He endeared himself to all of us not only with his Shakespeare but also with his ability to sing. He was so good at it, we always asked him to sing for us. He was as good in being friendly as he was firm, when he had to be. Even after decades, we were not sure if we learnt good English from him, but we sure learnt to appreciate good songs.

In spite of all the fun in the classroom, I continued to feel that I should have gone to the IIT instead of the state-run college. Some of my friends did get into IIT Madras, which had a 100 acres campus, just opposite to our tiny property. I would go once a month to meet my friends for a sleepover in their dorms and enjoy the ambience of IIT.

It looked like a different world, and the students were obviously very bright. They would talk of some strange name called Erwin Schrödinger and much stranger-sounding branch of physics called quantum mechanics. This was not taught in our college as our syllabus was set different. And how I missed all of it! I should have been there studying those esoteric subjects!

Driven by the urge to be somebody other than who I was, I decided to teach the quantum theory to myself. That way, I would know what the IIT students learnt without being a part of that institution. How and where would I get the books used by the professors in IIT?

The US Information Service had a spacious library in Madras and was attractive for two reasons. One, it had excellent books, and two, it was free for any student of any college in the city. That membership was promptly procured, and I was there every weekend, poring over the rows of books that lined that beautifully designed library.

That was where I met with my sci-fi gurus, Isaac Asimov, and George Gamow. They took me to meet other all-time physics greats Pauli, Dirac, De Broglie, Schrödinger, Einstein, Bose, Feynman, and so many others. The thirty years of their physics that shook the world in the early part of twentieth century was clearly shaking me up now. The quantum bug truly got into me as a consequence and soon was dominating my subconscious. I somehow began to dream of myself as an Einstein. Heisenberg danced in my dreams. Louis de Broglie laughed with me. Sir C. V. Raman smiled at me. It was a quantum carnival inside my head.

As I struggled to gain some understanding of the Feynman lectures, a thought flashed into my head. What if I proved Einstein wrong? Would it not be a game changer, something not done since the time Einstein walked on earth? Would it not catapult me ahead of so many other bright minds? For someone in a mighty hurry, this looked like a perfect solution. At that young age and being desperate, not once did it occur to me that it was silly!

Where would I begin to beat Einstein? It had to be a path-breaking area for which he got recognised; that would have the maximum impact. This set me thinking feverishly, and soon enough I realised Einstein won the Nobel Prize not for the complicated relativity theory, but for the conceptually path-breaking, and yet very simple, photoelectric effect theory. I had to something in this field, I concluded.

Einstein had proved that light was not a wave after all by his photoelectric effect discovery, turning centuries of understanding about light upside down. All along, it was accepted that a visible light was but a train of electromagnetic waves. Einstein's discovery must have bugged Maxwell real hard, who was so proud of his wave theory. 'How about returning the favour to Einstein by proving him wrong? But how?' I mused.

When light travels from one medium to another, Maxwell's electromagnetic theory tells us that wavelength changes but frequency remains constant; only the phase velocity changes while group velocity stays same, according to Einstein's theory. 'What if frequency also changed?' I asked myself. Group velocity would change and the velocity of photon would change! That would be something!

Now it felt like I was the boy Einstein looking at the ray of light streaming in from a church window, asking if the particles would look stationary. Excepting, I wanted to prove him wrong.

I kept chasing this ghost in my spare time in the beginning.

Very soon, this genie devoured me, and I was practically spending all my time thinking about this. I brought in slabs of different glasses, dunked them in water, and flashed so many coloured light sources and made all kinds of observations. I worked on reams of paper, trying the entire math I knew and this went on for a couple of years before I finally managed to write a paper.

While all this was going on, we moved into the third year of our degree, the year we started our specialisation in the selected major. And yes, I did get into electronics major and felt a wave of relief to get away from the cycloids and chemistry.

Now that I had a paper ready, I took my crazy idea to one professor after another, and they did not know how to react. There they were, in a government college, doing their job to earn a living, and this young student was bothering them with a fancy hypothesis of proving Einstein wrong, which they could not deal with. Very soon they came to recognise that the best thing they could do was to refer me to someone else, who could understand what I was saying and even prove me wrong. They decided to send me to *Mat Science* institute.

The *Mat Science* institute was set up by the federal government to promote research in advanced mathematics and theoretical physics. Our dear physics professors suggested that I take my earth-shaking theory there.

I was very excited at the opportunity of standing in front of a group of scientists who were hobnobbing with CERN, the Max Planck Institute and Lawrence Livermore Labs. And that too for what? To challenge Einstein's theory. My professor who set up the meeting was a jolly good person. His attitude towards me was a bit ambivalent, moving from admiration to pity. He admired me for the courage I had to challenge Einstein, and he pitied me for the very same reason—challenging Einstein. He advised me to take this seriously and prepare well, as the scientists in *Mat Science* were famous for being brusque to the point being rude.

Prepare I did. The D-Day came, and I was ready. The meeting was scheduled in the afternoon, and so I went to my college as usual, attended the classes, and went to the smithy shop practical, where we forged and welded. We had to wear a khaki dress as the furnaces shot up a lot of soot and smoke. We all took enormous pride in getting dirty and showing off our shirts wet with sweat.

This done, I borrowed a bicycle from my friend and pedalled my way to the Institute. It was located in an isolated place, as though the society pushed the physicists to the edge of the city. The average men and these scientists would literally talk different languages, and it showed.

I walked in, wearing a sweaty and sooty khaki dress, with no scholarly looks or bagful of papers. The scientists were bewildered and shocked, but were polite enough to let me speak. The chalkboard was so large that it looked like an IMAX screen for me. 'Einstein assumes that velocity of light is a constant in any medium in his relativity theory. As light exhibits matter wave duality, he assumes group velocity does not change but only phase velocity changes to satisfy the electromagnetic wave theory. What if the group velocity also changes with change in refractive index of the medium like the phase velocity?' I went on and on. The problem was that I was talking conceptually without any horrendous equations.

In ten short minutes, the scientists stopped me and opined that while they appreciated my interests in theoretical physics, but would I please back up the startling hypothesis with some rigorous math? Having delivered the supreme judgement, they all got up and walked away, leaving me standing, harbouring a bruised ego. Einstein was saved from me, after all.

There went my hypothesis, and I was heartbroken. I could not even last for ten minutes of their questioning? I picked my bruised ego and pedalled way back to my anvil in the smithy shop. A hex nut head was waiting to be forged, and I had to forge my broken ego along with it!

If the institute of *Mat Science* wanted me to get some rigorous math to back my hypothesis, I sure would oblige. So I delved deep into complexities of quantum mechanics, borrowed more quantum theory books from the American Library, and read them till my head exploded. Any amount of pushing myself or rushing things up was not helping. I was getting more stuck and far worse, regressing.

However much I tried, I could not get a rigorous theory that the *Mat Science* wanted. Some sort of serendipity was called for. I was eagerly looking for it, even though looking for serendipity made it oxymoronic. After all, 'serendipity' by definition meant it would be a pleasant, unexpected discovery. If I was looking for it, how could it become unexpected?

By now, we had gotten into our junior year and the format of the classes changed. There were more seminars than before, not just classroom sessions. We were called upon to select a complex theory and present it to the class.

My selection was matter wave theory—what a big surprise!

That was when it happened, the chance to meet Umesh, my senior at college. He was a legend and moved around the campus like a ghost. Very tall, very fair, always dressed in white trousers and white slack shirt, his face shone like a radiant sun with intelligence and wisdom. His eyes shone like diamonds, with ferocious intensity of intelligence. The village gossip was that he had already submitted multiple papers in advanced control systems, satisfying the requirements for a PhD programme while being an undergrad student.

As I headed to the lectern to deliver my class seminar on wave matter duality, he walked in with a few of his friends. There was commotion in the class as all the assembled faces turned towards him in anticipation. Umesh had a reputation of asking very difficult and tricky questions in classrooms. So what would he ask today? This was on everyone's mind as well as mine. I introduced the idea of matter and waves in physics, talked about how light, which was a wave, sometimes cheated by behaving like a particle; then I narrated an incident from Einstein's life.

"When Einstein was a liitle boy, he saw rays of scattered light falling in through the large colored windows in a cathedral. He imagined himself to be a light particle and realised that light would appear stationary if he moved at the same speed" The audience loved this story and I kept looking at Umesh, wondering when he would launch his barrage of questions. He kept smiling indulgently at me; so far so good.

Then I broke into Louis De Broglie's matter wave equation that said it was now the turn of matter to behave like a wave; electrons behaved like a wave. One could compute wavelength by dividing Planck's constant by the momentum of electrons.

The much-awaited thing then happened. Umesh stood up and asked, 'Is this valid for any reference frame and for any group of electrons?' On my answering in the affirmative, he followed with the question: 'Am I a DC generator then, since my relative velocity with respect to earth is zero?'

I stumbled a bit and wondered why he had asked that; then I got it. Since my relative velocity with respect to earth was zero, dividing the Planck's constant by zero results in infinity. A DC voltage is mathematically equivalent to a wave with infinite wavelength. Very clever!

For the next few minutes, there was a lot of arguments going back and forth between us bordering on relativity theory and quantum mechanics. Needless to say, this was totally lost on the audience, but what was not lost on them was that I was being cut to pieces and put on mat. For them, it did not matter if they were able to follow the conversation or not; they sure followed that Umesh was having fun at my expense, and they had the ringside seat watching the fun. They just loved it.

Then Umesh got up and left with his friends, as abruptly as he had come in. The class disbanded, and everyone filed out with great satisfaction. They looked like the Romans walking away from a coliseum after witnessing the Christians being eaten alive by the lions. They pretended that I did not exist, rather that I should not exist. Needless to say, I gladly reciprocated the feeling.

I would not meet Umesh again for a very long time. When I finally would meet him again, he would have a permanent effect on me. He would take me to a wizard of a man, a guru for the world, a person whose kindness knew no bounds, one who turned my world upside down with very few words spoken. He would launch me into a lifelong journey and a quest to find myself and the true nature of this universe.

I was yet to meet the challenge thrown by the mad scientists of *Mat Science* institute. Suffice it to say that when you are in mad hurry, you tend to go in all directions, without any coherent purpose. First, your desire to get somewhere drives you, and pretty soon, the momentum of search takes over and you lose control. Particularly, if you don't know what you are searching for. Like it is when you are searching for serendipity.

My search for the serendipity was still on. Then someone suggested I should get in touch with one Prof. George Sudarshan, a brilliant quantum theorist who was teaching in Harvard, Syracuse, and Tata Institute, among others.

George Sudarshan was a legend, a philosopher-physicist who pioneered the V-A theory of weak forces. Richard Feynman is recognized for using that theory a lot and was so respectful of him. In his view, the famous theory was discovered by Sudarshan and Marshak, and all he did was to partner with Gell-Mann and publicise that. Feynman was large hearted enough to recognize the greatness of Sudarshan, even if it meant a bit of reduced glory for himself. He straddled the intellectual firmament like a blaze and was as comfortable with physicists like Feynman as he was with abstract philosophers like Jiddu Krishnamurthy, popularly called as JK.

I decided that he would be the final arbiter in my quarrel with Einstein.

With all excitement, I sent my paper to him and waited with bigger anxiety to hear from the great physicist. The physicist did not respond but the philosopher sure did. George was caring enough to write a reply which was full of advice. He asked me to make a clear choice between being a theoretical physicist or a practical engineer. According to him, I could not be both.

'Mind you,' he said, 'being a theoretical physicist meant being absolutely lonely, literally and figuratively. It might take a lifetime to get some fame, if any at all, and most certainly no fortune at the end of the career. Unless you won a Nobel Prize.' I got the message and understood that chances of me winning a Nobel Prize as an amateur physicist were only slightly better than being able to grow wings and fly to the moon in a day.

I decided to listen to George and stop chasing quantum theory. But like we always do, I did not want to listen to good advice completely either. I mused, 'Who knows? The guy whom even Richard Feynman respected did not understand me fully. What if I had a genius hiding in me of some other variety, which he could not detect?'

Like Botany, for example.

Yes, it had to be electrical activity in plants. It was different from physics, and yet related to physics. It opened up opportunities of experimenting without the need for horrendous mathematical equations. 'I don't have to worry about the mad scientists of the *Mat Science*,' I thought. The only regret was that Einstein would go free. 'Maybe I could get Maxwell instead.'

If not the matter scientist, why not the wave scientist? My head started racing, and soon it came out with another crazy hypothesis. I could not prove Einstein wrong, but would leverage the works of J. C. Bose. He was the Indian botanist who did pioneering work on electrical activity in plants. I wondered, 'Why not combine Maxwell's electromagnetic theory and Bose's theory? How about inducing plants to act as antenna to receive broadcast TV signals?'

Pretty soon, I developed a hypothesis and a detailed paper.

Next, I had to find out a university that would be willing to examine that, without asking for a complex mathematical rigor. *Mat Science* was still haunting me. A quick research yielded a lead—the University of Agricultural Sciences. It was reputed and had a very large campus and a much larger endowment. And it is in the city of Bangalore, the land of Nobel laureate C. V. Raman and the Indian Institute of Science.

And so off to Bangalore I went, taking my paper along to meet the scientists researching the plants. The University of Agricultural Sciences had a long driveway with a well-manicured lawn in the front. Beautiful roses adorned the garden; every inch was a literal endorsement of the purpose of the institution. As it happens in all large establishments, the buildings were unduly large, and I was ushered into an ugly, large classroom where the agriscientists were waiting.

I started explaining the electrical activity in plants and how we could create a method of tuning them to receive electromagnetic waves. I slowly built up the theory behind it, outlined the applications, and listed the cost benefits. It was going well, and I began to feel better of myself. 'Maybe this time will be different,' I thought.

No, not really. They listened to me politely and carefully but with the now-familiar disbelief. After some encouraging words, the advice was the same; I should make up my mind if I wanted a scientific career or engineering. I should not aim for both. They cannot be combined.

This was as much intriguing as it was disappointing. Why was there a viewpoint among scientists that engineering was practical and hence lowly, while science was out of the world and hence holy? Was it not true that engineering is based on science and hence as holy?

Was this a way society over compensated for long periods of scientists being forced to recant by the churches? Like the tormented becoming the tormentors in future?

We cannot prevent scientific theories from becoming practical applications over a time. Unless of course, we make it that way by creating an artificial value in being valueless. It was simply unacceptable to me, and so I would make one more attempt at something which was scientific but closer to engineering.

American success stories about scientific inventions becoming a great business venture were driving me crazy. Do we say that Edison's engineering inventions were not based on science? Or did Armstrong walk on moon leaving science back in the world as the rockets blasted off? Did Magellan use astrology and not science when he circumnavigated the world? I was pretty certain it was not the case.

'Maybe the third time was my charm,' I thought, and kept looking for another breakthrough idea that would not be a hypothesis or a paper but would be a practical application. By this time I was in the junior year, and I would graduate with a bachelor's degree in a year. What would I do after graduating?

Like all college kids, it was a group thing. It was always about what 'we would be doing once the college days are over'. It was never about what 'I would do', even though it was clear to everyone that each will have to face the life alone.

Five of us in the class had jelled as a gang of 'glass mates', all studious, nerdy, and wearing spectacles. We five—PMJ, VKJK, Kamesh, Naren, and myself—were an odd gang with a very unusual mix of outlook. We came from very diverse backgrounds, but somehow we bonded together and were always seen together.

'P. M. Jay' was clearly the bonding agent who was so good in creating situations that brought all of us together. He was the best student of the class and the whole university. He was always pleasant, cheerful, and focused on identifying and going after what was good for him. He set clear objectives for life, and as his life evolved, he went on to do his management graduation, landed in America, and made it big.

'VKJK' Jayakumar was the funniest guy and very humble. His father was the top bureaucrat in the state government and his sister-in-law was a federal political leader and a minister in the cabinet. But he would not show off. His ability to make every one laugh was unbelievable, and he could keep one laughing forever. His life's journey also took him to America.

Kamesh was the simplest of the lot, coming from a typical middle-class family. His father was a traditional, orthodox priest, who lived a very simple life. Kamesh was a genuine guy, whose commitment to his family, respect for his parents, and love towards everyone was exemplary. He would also land up in America, which he would give up to be with his old parents in India.

'Naren' Narayanan was the complex piece of the puzzle. Very focused, bright, and occasionally aloof, Naren was the adult of the gang. Very tall and lean, he matched VKJK in humour. After plenty of globetrotting, he would also settle down in America.

Me? I was a drifting gyroscope, spinning wildly and wobbling without direction—seemingly in a hurry to get somewhere fast, but getting nowhere in particular. This was a big contrast with other 'glass mates', as they appeared to lead their lives in measured steps, looking almost certain where they were heading.

There were a few girls in our college, which was by itself a rarity. A couple of girls were part of our circle, 'Jyo' Jyoti and 'Shy' Sheila. They were extremely dignified, studious, always competing with Jay for the top rank, and winning our respect. Jyoti would blossom into a national-level top scientist, and Sheila would be a decorated professor, both earning PhDs.

My friends called me 'our own Einstein' affectionately, a bit ironic considering I was working hard to prove Einstein wrong. It goes to prove that friends are always kind to you, no matter what you are or will be. They continued to egg me to keep trying and not lose faith in myself, in spite of *Mat Science* and University of Agricultural Sciences setbacks. And they were also getting a bit impatient as they realised that their horse was chasing all other horses, rather than the win post.

I continued to work hard, but I always wondered what the winner hypothesis would be.

As we progressed towards our final year programme, there were frequent seminars and projects. We had to spend lots of time in the libraries than in classrooms. It was just as well, as I was spending most of time in libraries anyway, 'cutting classes' as it was called then. We all had to find a topic, develop a hypothesis, and if possible, build a working model and present it. There was very little funding available, and hence many chose theoretical paper projects.

Not me; I had to be different and original and researched a lot. I came out with an idea which I christened 'The Delta Antenna'.

The black-and-white TV was introduced in India just then, and like everywhere else in the world, it was a great status symbol to own a TV before your neighbours did. Those were the days of 'broadcast only' TV; there were no cable channels, and the state owned the broadcast stations.

You needed a dipole antenna mounted on the rooftops to receive the dull and boring programmes. This was commonly known as a 'Yagi' antenna, named after the Japanese inventor. The Yagi brought Bollywood songs and movies down to everyone's living room. The antenna became the most popular thing in everyone's life, just after religion.

These antennas were made of an aluminium tube with a dipole at the centre, with directors and reflectors on either side. In those days of licences and permits, aluminium mining and tube drawing were restricted by a quota system controlled by the government. There was a scarcity that drove the price high. The Yagi antenna cost quite a bit, and those with more number of elements gave a better reception and naturally cost more. More the elements, more the aluminium; more the aluminium, more the costs—that was how the equation worked.

'What can we do to reduce the cost of a Yagi antenna?' I asked myself. I did not have to look very far for the answer. It was just staring at me—reduce the aluminium content in the aluminium antenna!

How does one reduce aluminium content in an aluminium tube?

My friend Maxwell was ready with an answer. His famous electromagnetic wave theory explained it. Frankly, he had been shouting the answer from the rooftops (pun intended), but no one was listening. No one but for me, now.

Let us hear what Maxwell's got to say. In simple terms, Maxwell's electromagnetic waves theory states that the waves in the sky induce currents only to a shallow depth as they fall on metal surfaces. The depth of penetration depends on material type and the frequency of radiation. This meant that for the TV signal radiations, the Yagi antenna made of aluminium tubes would have the current flowing through only for a very small depth. A very small depth in this game meant about a few microns or a fraction of a thou or mil. A micron is a millionth of millimetre. This is called 'skin depth'.

This meant, only a very insignificant part of the aluminium tubes were really needed. So why did they build Yagi antennas with considerably thicker tubes of several tens of mils?

That was because the manufacturers could not make such thin tubes as they were structurally weak and would not stand. 'Pray,' they would ask themselves, 'how would a tube with thickness of fraction of mil stand firm without structural rigidity?' And they would shake their heads gravely as those who think they know the best usually do.

Not me, who was fond of proving even Einstein wrong. 'What if we take a plastic tube or wooden tube and electroplate it with aluminium?' I asked myself. Electroplating process deposits metals on substrates to a controlled, fine thickness of a few mils. So we could have a lightweight yet sturdy antenna with just adequate metal to just to cover the skin depth. Voila!

I called it 'delta' antenna, as the Greek letter delta is the symbol used for skin depth calculation using Maxwell's equations. It looked like I finally got all my ducks in a row. I now had something which was scientific, theoretical, and with a practical applications. *Mat Science* scientists or George Sudarshan could not stop me any more. The only thing I needed to do was to get to our electrochemical lab and get the delta antenna built. As simple as that. So I thought.

It was mid-1970s, and there were not many entrepreneurs around in India. It had to be tried out only in our college laboratories. The trouble was that the government institutions were not famous for innovations or risk-taking either. They were just doing their jobs and going home. It was next to impossible to convince the professor of the electrochemical lab to try the delta antenna. But, I had no other option and had to try with the professor of our lab.

I literally had to climb great heights to try convincing him that it was a worthwhile project. The professor was very proud of his biggest project ever done in the college—an electroplated large FRP water tank.

It was literally the showpiece, standing tall, holding hundreds of gallons of water, for everyone in the sprawling campus to see.

He took me to the top of the tank to show off his achievement. I needed his help, so I just went along and climbed a very long flight of steps. It was a cast iron ladder leading to the tank some 150 feet above the ground. He kept talking, and I kept following him and we reached the top. Never did I realise that it could be so windy up there and it was, throwing us almost out of balance. The large tank was open and filled with some twenty feet of water.

The good professor joked that if we fell down in the tank, no one would know. 'No one would miss you either,' I muttered to myself, as he was so unpopular in his class. As we started climbing down, he slowly expressed his inability to support the project. 'We just don't have that kind of money to spend on experimental projects. Nor do we have any authority to do anything other than the curriculum,' he politely explained. It seemed to me that he was enjoying my disappointment.

This plan did not work as expected. 'What should I do next?' I kept wondering, until I heard of a crazy entrepreneur and his crazier wife. Apparently, I was wrong in thinking that there was a shortage of risk-taking entrepreneurs in India then. There were some who had got educated in America and had come back to India to try some new start-ups from a garage.

Not many owned cars then in India. But some would build a garage anyway and let them out to any barber shop.

This guy decided to start his own Yagi antenna shop in the garage, and as he was crazy brainy, he was supported by his wife in money management. The back-alley conversation was that he only knew how to spend on material and men, while she had to step out to collect for the deliveries made. It was but natural that she became crazier over a period of time.

This was a golden opportunity that I was not going to miss. One more duck was getting in the row! I tried to meet them to promote my idea of building the Yagi antenna with an FRP or wooden poles electroplated with aluminium. I called on them several times to explain the plan, but I could not get past his wife. She very quickly understood that my idea might take away any little sanity that was left in her husband and felt it was best not to let me meet him at all. A *wife's* call is always a *wise* call.

The delta antenna ended even before it started. Maxwell smiled and felt relieved. He too was safe from my crazy theories and me.

So it was back to square one, as they say. After chasing Einstein, electrical signals in plants, and electroplated wood, I was back where I started. All my efforts to break free from the mediocre existence were thwarted, and I did not know what waited for me next. As I was chasing all these crazy ideas, I focused away from the undergrad syllabus. I got distracted and lost out in grades.

I was scoring a first class in Indian grading system, equivalent to a B score in the United States. This was simply not good enough in a job market with unemployment running at double digits. My attempts at being an amateur scientist became a recipe for disaster.

It was the summer vacation before we stepped into the final year. It was time for all of us students to go on an all-India tour, ostensibly for visiting companies to learn how the practical world worked. It had plenty of sightseeing thrown in on the side.

Sixty of us left by train, with a coach reserved all for ourselves. We chugged along to Bombay, Delhi, Chandigarh, Hyderabad—and on the side, we visited Ajanta caves, Shimla hill resorts, Agra fort, and Taj Mahal. We lived mostly in the coach, as it lay shunted at the 'outer' in many places. This way we did not have to spend money for any lodging!

The factories, products, and the boring talk we got during the tour did not interest me. It bothered me a lot that in spite of working myself out in a mad rush, I was not making any progress. Rather, I was going backwards, scoring a B grade, while being recognised as the 'Einstein' of the class. And here I was, listening to some old man explaining how class C amplifiers generated high amplification in the transmitter. It was not at all clear what I would be doing after graduating.

'What was going wrong?'

This persistent thought was acting a like a wound spring, driving me into unfocused hyperactivity. It made me petulant, and I troubled the supervisors with irrelevant questions. It made me try to climb a steep rock of forty feet in Ajanta—without any formal training or equipment—and get stuck in the middle of the climb, not knowing how to climb down or go up, giving a scare to watchers below. It caused me to walk alone at the Taj Mahal when everyone was together with their loved ones.

In short, I was all alone, even in a crowd, wandering aimlessly.

How were my 'glass mates' doing? Jay was hitting the top ranks, planning his grad school in management and further move on to the United States. So were VKJK and Naren. Kamesh was clear where he stood and had drawnhis plan for working for a couple of years and doing master's in engineering.

Complicating matters further, my mind was moving in another direction that would rewire my entire life. I was getting drawn more towards my senior friend Umesh, who was more than just a bright student. He was a true yogi. He took me on a journey that would make me wade through nearly 5,000 years of thought process that dominated the region between the Danube and the Indus.

It was more adventurous than white water rafting and more rewarding than anything else in the whole world. It would take me to a person who knew how to teach without speaking a word, how to bring discipline without being harsh, and how to take one to one's destination without setting goals.

I sure was spinning around in a whirlpool.

Soon enough, the valedictory day arrived, and it was celebrated with all the due solemnity. Sombre things were told, songs were sung, and everyone shared their plans for jobs and graduate studies.

All but me; I had nothing to show or share. I had chased the ghosts of Einstein, Bose, and Maxwell and lost. They were all rolling in their graves, laughing at me. Confident that I would best them, I had not tried for any job position or graduate study and was marooned and stood there empty-handed.

As the celebrations, music, and dancing were on full swing, I staggered out of the event hall and walked around aimlessly till I reached the tree temple. The tree temple was a small affair, a small box-like structure with a small portrait of Hindu god Shiva. A small trident, the favourite weapon of Shiva was stuck on the ground. There was an apology of an oil lamp, and it was very dark at nights.

None of us ever saw any one praying at the outfit and hence the rumour mill was active that some sort of a strange yogi visited the temple at the dead of the night and prayed. My legs dragged me there, and I sat in front of the shoebox temple and started crying inconsolably.

'How can I be doing the true education, working hard night and day trying to innovate, and yet end up with a B and no job?' I wondered.

My friends could offer only sympathy, but none could offer solutions. Some even looked at me like I was an intelligent fool. If there was one friend who was very sure I would eventually succeed was our woman friend Jyo.

She was regal, quiet, and brilliant. She was always at the top ranks of the class and had a huge following. She was nice to others, and she always felt I would make it big one day, do something different from everyone else. It was comforting to know that. As the future unfolded, we would not meet each other for two decades. All her faith in me would turn up to be reasonably true.

Nothing seemed to be working for me, not even the final year project. I had teamed with another friend of mine who shared my burning desire to be innovative. We did not want to do any routine project, and so we hit upon the idea of making an implantable cardiac pacemaker that would be charged remotely. The idea was to radiate the charging power in IF band of radio waves using a square loop antenna that will be picked up by the IF receiver of the pacemaker. We dreamt that one day, we would have the receiver in the implanted pacemaker pick up the IF signals of the broadcast radio in the sky, convert to DC and charge the battery. All this, while the person was listening to his favourite music! Very clever, eh?

How do you test it? We were very sure that no sane living person would like testing it! At most, we could demonstrate that it worked on the lab table. Or maybe we could test it on a dog? Would the Blue Cross permit it? Or maybe the town would let us test it on a street dog they were planning to put down? We just did not know, and in our hurry to do something very different, we did not pause to get this important final testing sorted out. We just went ahead and completed a project that could not be tested.

So the implantable pacemaker remained a lab model admired by everyone, but we just would never find out if it worked in a living body, man or animal. Soon enough, we all graduated from college, bid our goodbyes, and went to our grad school or jobs. All except me, as I had neither. The scare finally started to sink in and made me miserable. I rushed back to my professor and asked if it was possible to get into the graduate programme MS. He knew me well and always was appreciative of my efforts to be innovative. He promised to take me in the grad programme of Communication Engineering if at least one of those registered dropped out.

It meant I was on wait list! Einstein baiter on a wait list? 'Well, even the great Einstein was rejected in the beginning,' I mused.

This was a wake-up call to get my act together. Here I was rushing to do so many things, probably without any focus or plan. Maybe my innovative urge was overwhelming me? Maybe I was trying to catch up with my well-to-do friends who had gone off to study in pricier IITs that I could not afford? What was clear to me was that when 'we are in a hurry, we should slow down'.

We should control the events and never ever let events control us. There is no need to prove anything to anyone, including one's own self. You must respect life and take it as it comes, just like the mountain climbers who respect the peaks they climb.

I learnt my lesson—*if you are in a hurry, slow down.* This lesson would come handy. Someone would drop out, and I would be offered the MS seat that I would graduate with distinction. I would get three jobs even before I finished my graduation, and a PhD admission from the prestigious Tata Institute in Bangalore.

This PhD admission was another hilarious story. It was more like a mock teaching session with role reversals, the professors sat as students and I was the Teaching Assistant asked to derive the famous Maxwell's equations from 'first principles'. Maxwell again!

Boy, did I get stuck so many times in the process, much to the amusement of the professors! As soon the interview was over, I was so depressed that I got into the next available train and rushed off home at Madras. I had done terribly and was very irritated to be welcomed by my family all in smiles, when I reached home. 'Don't they understand that I got walloped, mathematically speaking?' I thought.

It was not that at all; they showed me a telegram from the Tata Institute, admitting me into the PhD programme. Got admitted?

It looked like Maxwell was happy with me after all. Later it would be told to me that of all the candidates who were tested, I went furthest in deriving the equations, with none ever completing it. How did this come to happen?

All because I slowed down when I was in a hurry, planned, and focused.

Promptly, I plunged into the decision process. Having many things to choose from made the decision-making more difficult. Which one would I select? Would I accept the job as the R&D engineer in one of the largest electrical equipment manufacturers in India? Or the Class 1 bureaucrat engineer position in federal government? Or join the aerospace giant as a management trainee? Or join the PhD programme and harass Einstein or Maxwell again?

I decided to seek the advice and counsel from a totally unexpected source, from my yogi friend Umesh's guru. His Holiness Abhinava Vidya Theertha was head of the hoary institution established by the eighth-century philosopher Shankara. He had the ability to become what was needed, to make anyone who sought his guidance comfortable. He could be an abstract philosopher for the learned, a high priest for a priest, a kind benefactor for a devotee, and a tough administrator for officialdom.

He asked me two simple questions—what would I do after finishing my PhD, and whether I liked to deal with people or stuff.

'I would take a job of course,' I answered. 'Oh, yes, I really loved meeting and dealing with people.'

'Then you should take the management trainee position in the aerospace company.'

Like the bumbling idiot of the Tyre Rack ad, who crosses snow-clad mountains to meet a guru to ask which tyre he should choose, I crossed rivers and mountains to ask the guru, who led people to eternal happiness, how to choose my career. Although we rarely spoke with each other, I always listened to him.

At his prodding, I would learn yoga, meditation, and launch into one of the longest and enthralling learning cycle of my life. For the next thirty-five years, I would keep learning about the six disciplines that characterised traditional Indian philosophical system and continue my regime of yoga and meditation.

He silently and mysteriously guided me to understand yet another paradox in life—*to get something you cherish, you should learn give up what you already have.*

IF YOU WANT SOMETHING,
GIVE UP WHAT YOU HAVE.

CHAPTER 3

❧

Listening to Guru's Silence

We generally understand that listening involves our directing attention to someone else talking and absorbing all the words being spoken. While we understand that paying attention is very relevant, it is not very clear if what is said about absorbing the words spoken is very right. In fact, oftentimes it is more difficult to listen and absorb the words when some is talking. We can sure hear them, but listening is another matter.

The problem is the *words*. We are trained to believe that words have a meaning, while, in fact, they don't have any innate meanings. They are *arbitrarily given* meanings by convention. It is very well known that the same words *imply* different things to different people, depending on their world views, even if the meaning is understood to be the same.

What a speaker is always trying to do is share his/her ideas and transpose the understanding somehow to the recipients. If the words contribute to confusion, we can conceptually relate to a view that any 'non-wordy' method is likely to better. Extrapolating this strain of argument, we can conclude that *communicating through silence* is the best way.

The trick is to know how to do it. My guru was a master of that skill—a smile now, a nod there, and couple of words now and then. And what is more important, always empathising with your failures and making it light on expectation. All this, after helping you understand the relevance of higher goals to achieve.

The only thing we had to do was to learn to listen to his silence during the several visits we made individually and as a group. We were a motley bunch of friends led by Umesh, who attracted a highly educated lot who were desperate to reconnect with ancient philosophic concepts developed by the Vedic Aryans.

The guru in Sringeri was perhaps a high school dropout in early 1950s' when he decided to become a monk. But he sure knew how to connect with us who all came with master's and PhD degree in engineering decades later. On one rare occasion when all the four *shankaracharyas* of the nation congregated in Sringeri, he proudly pointed to all of us and told them that his disciples were all masters at the minimum. He sure knew how to be the right thing to every one.

I tried my best to listen to his silence. Most of my visits to his ashram involved me just sitting in a corner and watching him, listening to his conversations with others.

Following the advice of the guru, I accepted the offer of the aerospace company's management trainee programme.

The aerospace company had a hoary past; it was started by a visionary industrialist Walchand Hirachand in the early 1940s. He was a pioneer in many ways; he started India's first modern shipyard, first car factory, and the first aircraft factory. It was manufacturing advanced fighter jets, helicopters, and avionics systems for the Indian Air Force.

The programme was designed and delivered in collaboration with IIT for production technology and IIM for production management. These were national-level institutes and were considered equivalent to MIT and Harvard. This was a much sought-after programme—for every candidate selected, hundreds were rejected.

It was also a crazy programme in which we had to study seventeen subjects in a year, covering all aspects of aircraft design and manufacturing. The company was trying to make us wizards of aircraft production technology in such a short time. A well-intended thought but it played out very hard on me, who came in with master's in electronics. Imagine a guy like me who spent years studying electromagnetic waves theory and fighting with Maxwell being asked to understand a strange-sounding 'aero-thermodynamics of turbo machinery'! I did not know who suffered more, myself or the professors who struggled to make me understand.

The programme was run by a retired full colonel from Indian Army. 'Old habits die hard,' they say. This fine gentleman was no exception, and he ran our residential course in true armed forces tradition. We had to wake up early at the crack of the dawn, do our physical exercises, shave clean, take a shower, dress up, and show up in the mess with shiny polished shoes. The butlers (*yes butlers*!) had the right to refuse us entry if they found us shabby enough. It was all knives and forks in British style. In the evening, we had to play volleyball or go for a swim.

All along, I continued to learn from my guru's silence; I continued to visit his ashram, sit silently, and watch as he taught other disciples in Sanskrit, the language of the gods.

It would dawn on me much later that all the knowledge was inside our brains, waiting to be discovered, and languages were, in fact, a hurdle. The fastest way to acquire knowledge was through the awareness process rather than the learning process. May be the guru was training me in this through his silence. It was always through a smile, a look, a frown, and just a couple of words, and it conveyed all the meaning to me.

One day, I heard him patiently explain some nuance of Shankara's philosophical work to a scholar who appeared agitated over the counterpoints of a rival philosopher. The scholar somehow felt that the other guy sounded more right than his beloved Shankara. And yet he was not willing to accept the competing view.

It would have been easy and normal for my guru to dismiss off the competing view, talk gloriously of Shankara, reiterate the mythology of him being an avatar of Shiva, and suggest that the scholar must reject the other view. After all, he was leading an institution established by Shankara himself.

Not my guru, who clearly saw himself more as a guru than a pontiff of a church. He admonished the scholar for not pursuing his enquiry in an honest manner. If the scholar felt that the competing view was more acceptable, he should move on and embrace that. Else the whole philosophical enquiry becomes a dogma, a religion based on beliefs rather than understanding.

It was another matter, he thundered, that he could reconcile and explain why Shankara made more sense. But it was for the scholar to find that out in an honest manner.

'You need to prepare yourself to give up what you have to get what you seek,' he declared, closing the conversation, and he gave a side glance at me and smiled. As if he used the context to actually guide me rather than the scholar.

It was a clear instruction and a framework for any seeker in any field. If we cling to our existing belief or current facts, our quest for truth will come to an abrupt end. Truth is an aggregate of many facts, some of which may not contribute to the Truth. Why so?

Psychologists tell us that knowledge is an intersection of truth and belief system, with Truth being an aggregate of many facts. Yet, *we parade our knowledge as facts*. We should be prepared to drop them if we want to move forward. This is true for any pursuit, be it science, economics, management, or whatever.

This was very helpful in my journey over next fifteen years, in which my career took me to be so many different things. I would be a CNC machine shop engineer, avionics engineer, system analyst, sales leader, a CIO, COO, and a quality leader driving the legendary Jack Welch's vision of making six sigma the way we work.

No two consecutive roles were similar, never allowing me to build on my previous experience. It was not possible to embrace new roles, without being able to discard the mould of the previous one. At every change, I could mentally visualise my guru nodding his head appreciatively. But all this came about after a difficult adjustment period and learning in practice.

The training programme was bothering me a lot as I continued to believe that I was a communication systems engineer and not an aircraft engineer. Why was I being asked to study all those subjects that have no relevance to what I am or what I want to be? The much-dreaded cycloids and engineering drawings began to roar their heads again with vengeance. In fact, with so many subjects to learn, they seemed to have actually grown into hydra-headed monster!

I continued to resist learning new stuff during the one-year stay at IIT Madras, and it showed in the results. I very nearly flunked as the minimum pass grade was 60 per cent. The only thing I enjoyed was trying to learn swimming in the evenings and playing volley ball in the mornings. Clearly, I had not paid attention to my guru as he was explaining the subtleties of a quest to the scholar.

When we moved to the company's corporate training school in Bangalore after a year, it was totally different. I very much enjoyed the management classes taught by the faculty of IIM Bangalore. I loved the ideas, loved the business games that we had to play; it felt terrific when we had to deliver impromptu seminars frequently. The monsters went back into hibernation.

Those management programmes were designed to test our ability to think differently. This became apparent when our professor called us out and said, 'You guys will have to find a unique topic, not covered in the class sessions, and deliver a short speech on that tomorrow. So good luck with your evening party plans!' He smiled at us meaningfully and left us to wonder. What would our topic be?

I spent hours devouring the racks of books to find a unique topic called 'management by irrationality'. It touched upon real-life problems managers face—how to decide without comprehensive and meaningful data? The hypothesis advocated was to break down the entire decision tree into a hierarchy of binary decisions, toss a coin at every level, call out heads or tails, and choose accordingly. I was very sure that this would provoke a big debate and hence would be well received.

My talk set the whole class into peals of laughter. Were they laughing at me or just found the speech hilarious? Since there were no meaningful data on their response, I decided that the audience simply loved it without even tossing a coin!

And then there was another talk of mine on 'Kings and Cabbages', and I sent the whole class rolling on the floor the way I told the story of how they were interconnected. I was winning and was becoming cocky.

Very soon, the class got their chance to take sweet revenge on me, and the way it happened was so embarrassing and an ego buster for me.

'Do you know what happens when you pass a message from one person to another in a chain? Do you think that the final person in the chain gets the undistorted message?' asked our organisation behaviour professor. There were peals of laughter in the classroom with many of nodding our heads sagely. Not content with this, he wanted to make his point through a small role play game.

'Here is what we will do. I will send away ten of you out of this classroom. The rest of you will see a short video clip with no dialogues. I will select one of you as the spokesperson. I will call one of the ten "out" standing team back into the class as the "listener". The selected spokesperson will have to explain the story of the video clip to the listener. Then, the second "out" standing guy will be called in, and the first guy will have to explain to him. This will go on till the last of the ten gets to hear the story from the ninth.' There was a big commotion in the class.

'I am not done yet.' He continued, 'The only condition is that at any given time, the conversation could only happen between the "communicator" and the "listener", with the rest of the class allowed only to laugh but not participate in the process. No crosstalk, no clarifying shouts. Are you game?'

Of course we were, and a great expectation engulfed the classroom. Something funny was sure going to happen.

The chosen ten strolled out, and the professor showed the video. It had a boy rowing a boat on the river Thames, the camera slowly zooming in to show a mosquito biting his right arm. The camera zoomed in further to the point of showing a tiny drop of blood oozing out due to the bite. Then, the camera zoomed out so far ahead that the entire universe was shown on the screen. Finally, the camera zoomed to normal level, and the boy rowed back to the shore. No dialogues whatsoever.

The professor knew about my background well and hence chose me to start the communication chain; after all, I had a master's degree in communication systems, didn't I? Was it not my complaint all along that they were trying to convert a communications engineer into an aircraft guy?

The first person was called in, and I started explaining the video, and he kept asking all sorts of probing questions that were so irrelevant. In my eagerness to get it right, I kept over-explaining, which made the guy ask more irrelevant questions. The class was laughing its wits out.

Then, the second guy was called in, and the first guy did worse than me; this continued till the ninth guy told the tenth guy a bizarre story.

'This boy got on to his boat moored on river Thames. He kept rowing till he reached Mars. There, he decided to test his blood, and much to his amazement he found that the haemoglobin content had shot up. The boy decided to row back to London to get it cured.' The tenth man told this with a deadpan face. It just did not make any sense even to him! The whole class went delirious and kept throwing accusing glances at me for having started the communication breakdown from 'get go'.

The proud communications engineer in me ran away, never to return.

With all the fun and fanfare, we completed our management training programme soon and were now due for an assignment into our first real-life job role. The company had a large avionics division, and with my master's in communications, I was very sure to be assigned to that unit. It just did not happen that way.

I was chosen to be the project engineer to set up a big CNC shop. The CNC machines were controlled by computers and were very sophisticated. It was a big disappointment and a scare for me too. I was never good at hands-on work, and now I had to manage a large shop? 'Maintenance work is for less qualified technicians, while I have two master's degree including management, so how dare they make me do this?' I said to myself. I was fuming in my mind.

Again, my unwillingness to let go *what I thought I had* in the interest of learning new things surfaced. And I took it up with the general manager. He would hear none of it. 'You will go where we assign you. We need someone well qualified to set this up as this is in the critical path of our project plan. Don't picture yourself as any engineer, which you are not. We are grooming you as leaders, and leaders don't flinch. Just go and do it.' He was a retired air force commander and just did not brook any disobedience. With a heavy and reluctant heart, I reported to my new manager in the maintenance department. He was a guy who had risen from the ranks and was considered to be a bully with particular dislike for young qualified professionals. I was obviously being thrown to a 'lion'.

'I don't want you in my department. Management trainees are spies of senior management, and I would have none of it. Please go back to the general manager and seek a transfer to some other department,' he snapped ignoring my proffered hand.

This was how my actual career started—with *a feeling of being unwelcome.*

And me? I always grew rapidly large internally any time I was challenged. This time was no different.

'If you don't want me, you go and request the general manager for the change,' retorted the larger me. 'I don't have any problem working for you, and so why should I?' He was dumbfounded, as he did not anticipate this response.

'Very well, then. I will make your stay here the most unpleasant experience of your life. Unwelcome to the department,' he said.

Looking back, my response appears surreal; how could a young employee retort that way to the first manager in his life? What was I thinking to retort that way?

This was an unusual start of my career, and my manager kept his word, making my life as much of hell as he could. He exploited one weakness we all have as we step out of our schools into the real world—*the difference between schools and real world.*

You did not get to see sophisticated and expensive machines in an engineering school those days, and hence you graduated with very little practical knowledge. This was truer for the state-run colleges that are run on shoestring budgets and fee waivers. For example, none of us could tell a hydraulics valve from an electric circuit breaker. Let alone troubleshoot complex problems, I was in no position even identify or locate components; I could not even correctly read an electrical layout diagram. To me, hydraulics sounded like a country cousin of the dreaded Frankenstein monster.

Engineering drawings were now taking their sweet revenge on me for having neglected them in the school. Those dreaded cycloids had patiently waited all these years and now declared war on me! I had to read big bad machine manuals to install or repair a machine, and those made no sense to me at all.

My manager knew this very well and exploited it very deftly. Being the most senior in rank, I was placed as the leader of the maintenance crew. They were experienced technicians, all very hands-on. All my manager had to do was to call my team and tell them not to 'cooperate with the new engineer'; he was but the management spy and so had to be avoided like the plague. The consequences played our terribly as anyone would easily predict.

Every time a machine went out of order, they would all come to me with a false respect and seek guidance, fully aware that I could give none. They would take me to the machine, with false politeness ask me to help out, and watch me fumble, unable to even locate the machine parts properly. I was becoming the laughing stock of the shop floor, with all machine operators inventing stories of the engineer who could not troubleshoot.

Pretty soon, they collectively declared that professional engineers were not best suited for the shop floor jobs. This was precisely what my manager was waiting for, and he struck.

My manager tried to get me out of the shop floor by complaining to the factory manager about my incompetence. 'My customers believe that he is unable to solve their problems. Not only the maintenance crew, but also the machine operators and shop supervisor are demanding a change,' started his long memo. He went on to list my misdeeds due to which he concluded that aircraft production programmes were getting impacted.

The factory manager was a retired field hockey player from the Indian Olympics team. He was known for the roughness typical of field sportsmen. He rejected the request with some unprintable words thrown in, matched with equally unprintable graffiti, and sent it back to my manager. He was tired of the games my manager had been playing for long and was perhaps waiting for someone like to me to take him head-on. He just refused to oblige.

How did we get to know? My manager's secretary had a field day gossiping about this graffiti, with several show-and-tell sessions. Everyone had a great laugh, but the graffiti did not solve my problem; it actually made it worse. It just managed to increase the hostility I was facing from my manager.

There were funny moments for me too. Like the day someone cleaned a dirty graduated scale of an inspection machine with a CTC (carbon tetrachloride) solution; the chloride ate away all the graduations, making the machine display all zeros only! Or another time, when a British engineer found that the CNC milling machine he was repairing was out of calibration, and wondered how we could produce aircraft-worthy parts. He kept scratching his head until he witnessed our weekly ritual worship of a Hindu goddess every Friday.

'It must be the gods and not the machine that produced parts for you,' he concluded.

We had another team of French engineers too, repairing French machines. They witnessed the reaction of the British engineers, and not to be outdone, they responded differently. They decorated the inside of the work cabinets with pin-up photographs, declaring them to be the goddesses *they* worshipped. Needless to say that many operators and technicians changed their religion and started worshipping the French goddesses!

Very soon I recognised that I needed to do some heavy lifting, something extraordinary to win the confidence of the machine shop workers. That had to be so different from the norm of the workmen. Time was running out, and the factory manager, our 'graffiti man', was losing patience with me.

I decided to study the entire company environment deeply and come out with a game plan.

The bureaucracy, lack of commitment, and lack of fire in the belly was truly appalling in that public sector enterprise. The employees excelled in the game of 'clock-watching'—everyone kept watching the clock, and at the stroke of shift closing, they just ran out of the gate to take the chartered bus home. The factory was left looking like a cemetery in the wee hours.

It is normal for factory workers to ride to work fresh early in the morning, to return tired and sleepy after a day's hard work. Not these workers, no sir! They would all ride the company bus sleeping in the morning, and be absolutely fresh, playing card games, as they ride back to work. They called themselves 'the five unches'. Why? Because they believed they were being paid for two 'punches' (in/out), a 'lunch', and two 'kunches' (kunchu is local language; it loosely translates to 'tea pot'). Not for working hard and producing airplanes!

Folks were blindly following a procedure without much of application of mind. The 'copper leg' incident demonstrated this. The security guards had gotten a tip that some workers were stealing expensive aircraft-quality copper wires by rolling them around the legs under the trousers. One culprit was caught 'red-legged', and the smart security guard took a snapshot of the leg (and *only the leg*), wound with copper wires. During the enquiry hearings, the concerned worker promptly declared that those were not his legs, and security could not prove it otherwise! What was the security thinking? That he was photographing Marilyn Monroe?

We had to contend not only with internal inefficiencies, but also the local government's. They were providing all the utilities services without much coordination with customers, resulting in a huge mismatch between demand and supply. For example, we were building our big machine shop while the local government did not have the capacity to deliver water or power.

We managed our power needs by having our own diesel-based generator set, but we just could not meet our water needs. Why was the water so important?

The computer-controlled numerical machines needed to be kept cool, failing which the computers went crazy and the machines malfunctioned. So the large machine shop was air-conditioned with a chilled water circulator, which was a very thirsty demon, gulping thousands of gallons of water every day. Government waterworks did not have the capacity to deliver that much water, and we did not have our own springs either. How did we feed the thirsty cooler?

We called for the local fire truck fully laden with water every day. They would arrive and park near the building; we would connect our water hose to the fire truck and carry the water hose to the top of the building; the chilled water plant had a water inlet there. Maybe it was a borderline legal thing and definitely a bad civic sense, but it worked. We continued to do this till the government utility caught up with the demand.

There were so many instances in which my ability to manage a terrible situation caused by the poor planning of my manager was challenged, which we solved with some native ingenuity. All the while, he was busy tracking me in his cross wire, ready to fire at one misstep. Slowly and steadily, the entire shop floor started recognising how I got things done, covering for my manager's inefficiency. The tide began to turn, and they started to appreciate me.

I gave up my pride, my ego, my memory of two master's degrees, and my management pedigree and worked wholeheartedly in their midst as their colleague. I was willing to get all dirty, greasing a machine bed, replacing the coolant, and getting under a machine to clean up, and drinking tea and eating with them. What is more important, as my guru wanted, I was willing to give up what I took pride in to get what I was seeking.

Things progressed to such an extent that I was able to analyse the problems and provide solutions merely by looking at manuals without even having to get near the machines.

The scales tilted, and I became the respected one. I started working two shifts, some fifteen hours a day, to learn more and get things done. My manager saw an opening in that, and he seized it.

The Department of Labour had enacted a Factories Act that had provisions to protect the labour from sweatshop conditions. One such provision called for a written prior approval from the factory manager, if any worker had to work for more than eight hours per day. Clearly, I had not taken a written permission for working so hard! My manager issued a citation to me, warning me of disciplinary action for violating the Factories Act. As per rules, he had to mark a copy to the factory manager, who was none other than our old 'graffiti man'. The graffiti man promptly threw this into the dustbin and issued a citation of his own, charging my manager of very poor planning! I was hailed a hero by the entire shop floor.

This catapulted me into fame and high visibility. My bonding with the maintenance crew was complete, and we worked hard, helping each other, stepping in for each other's deficiencies. The machine shop progressed fast to completion, and it was all buzzing in full speed. That most modern plant of that time looked like a robotics gallery.

This success brought me the rewards, and I was promoted as deputy manager and reassigned to the avionics lab to support flight trials. We were making several types of planes fitted with complex avionics systems that needed to be tested first in the simulator lab and then when they were in the planes as they flew. My new job was to head the crew that was carrying this out.

It was a pleasant irony of situation that in this deal, both my manager and I got what we wanted. He wanted me out and I wanted to be an avionics manager, and we both got our wish fulfilled.

My guru's wise advice had prevailed and helped me. I gave up what I thought I possessed, and in return I got what I was seeking. I was back now dealing with communication systems for advanced aircraft like fighters and transport and light helicopters, which was very much in line with the specialised master's degree I had.

This avionics job offered several opportunities to learn new things and solve problems in a difficult environment. The test pilots who flew the planes were a different breed; they had to literally put their life on line every time they took an unproven aircraft to flight.

They tended to be adventurous, brash, and occasionally brutal in their comments after a bad test flight. If our systems malfunctioned, we always got an earful and in slangs that we never understood. Their grumpy faces made it sure we understood they were not happy.

We had to be nimble, think on our feet, and quickly solve problems, as it was very expensive to keep an aircraft waiting on tarmac or hangars. The company lost so much money that it mattered even in our government-run establishment. We had to shed our ego, comforts, and whatever we thought was important for the only thing that mattered was solving the issues raised by the pilots.

Some of the problems were so unique that they manifested only in mid-air, not showing up during the ground test or in a flight simulator. The only way to get an understanding of those problems was to *fly with the test pilot*. Once airborne, the pilots believed they were growing wings of god and so they behaved. After all, they do defy gravity!

Us ordinary mortals were tagged along with them even to gain an understanding of what they were complaining of. We could not understand the problems on ground, let alone solve them. The daredevil pilots understood this clearly and played us to have their own fun.

Like that mischievous pilot who did the 'helicopter drop test' mid-air with me on board. The test called for cutting off the engine at an altitude, letting the rotors slow down to a particular speed, and starting the engine again. The engine was expected to start again and keep the helicopter afloat; if the engines stalled, we would all crash to earth like a rock. The pilot did that test several times that day, just to see me squirm in my seat in fear. He just loved it.

Or that very experienced AN 32 transport aircraft pilot, who took me on board to show me a noise problem. He not only made me stand all through the two-hour flight, but he also banked the large plane unusually sharp several times, making it near impossible for us to stand. His parting shot as we landed? That we should provide a flight engineer free for every set they bought!

This 'treatment' was reserved not only for us, the 'civvies', but also for the air force engineers. They were not pilots and hence did not qualify to be gods. We discovered that many of those air force engineers were wanting in technical expertise but had an abundant supply of posturing.

I once had a hilarious experience of being instructed by a squadron leader engineer when his big boss, the air commodore, was visiting the hangar. We were performing the ground test of avionic suite, when we heard the footsteps of the boss. The squadron leader looked up, counted the stripes of the air commodore, stood up, and gave a smart salute. He bellowed, 'Sir, I have instructed these civilians to test whatever they have to test and fix whatever that needs to be fixed, sir!'

I could not make what he was saying, but the air commodore seemed to have understood; he nodded his head appreciatively and walked away. We civilians tested 'whatever needed to be tested and fixed whatever needed to be fixed'. Just as the squadron leader commanded!

But then, we had another air force officer who was very knowledgeable and helpful. Wing Commander

Gosh was leading a team of engineers developing systems for advanced avionics. The system had powerful on-board computers connected together in a network. They did all the calculations needed for guiding the aircraft during its flight, identifying potential targets, and destroying them. He was understaffed and needed help. A couple of my pals and I decided to sign in to help him out and in that process build our expertise. Thus was born what came to be later called Smiths Trio ('Tridev' in short for triple developers)—Anil, Akhilesh, and myself. The bond we developed sustained for thirty years, not affected by inevitable separation and distance of thousands of miles.

This was a fortuitous move, as this brought us into the rarefied field of avionics system and software design. We were assigned different projects, and we worked hard to make an impact.

There were only a handful of people doing that kind of work anywhere in the world. We, the 'Tridev', were getting noticed by our senior management. This pulled us up in visibility and importance and in due course won us a place in a joint development effort that was being carried out in England. Smiths Aerospace was contracted by our company for development and production of advanced avionics system. We three were sent there to participate in the programme.

I was assigned to work in the systems analysis group. When I showed up at the manager's office, she welcomed me with a broad smile. 'Welcome to my team, Paddy, and I hope you will enjoy working with me,' said Judith Gibbins.

I was moved to tears. I had to wait five years and cross the seas to be welcomed on my first day at work!

Judith turned out to be a smart, tough, meticulous, and friendly boss for me. She was so supportive at work, letting me work on many projects, all the while throwing a protective net around me. She felt that was the best way to nurture new talent. At the same time, she never hesitated to shine the limelight or showcase any one of us when she felt we had done a great job.

The problem of 'air-to-air malfunction' during flight trials proved this beyond any doubt.

The weapon aiming computer was supposed to help the pilot to take aim and shoot down an airborne target with a gun. But in this flight trial, the system just did not work the way it should have; the gun traces were going all over except on target. Every one in the team was working hard to solve this problem, quite anxious and concerned that they will be drawn through hot coal by the chief engineer. I was left out from this.

'You are new, Paddy, and I don't want you to be listening to the tough talk John would give,' she consoled me. John was considered to be the brain of the design group. While Judith was protecting me, I just could not sit idle and watch every one else struggle. So I insisted she let me have go at it, but the offer was declined.

Taking a no for an answer was not my strength, and so I persisted. She reluctantly agreed to let me try. 'Here are the flight test reports and the software design documents. Try what you can do with this and get back to me.' With this advice, I was left to work on it.

Since the others were focusing on software and engineering aspects, I dived deep into the mathematics behind the algorithm. Soon enough, a glitch that was causing the problem was caught. Not content with just solving the problem, I went on to develop a new atmospheric model for tropical conditions and proved how it improved the aiming accuracy. Hesitantly, I took the results to Judith for her review. She quickly ran through the results and was overjoyed. 'I am happier for you than for myself. It is not always that a newcomer is able to solve problems that defy our efforts. This is the one for John. He has to know who solved this.' With this, she took me to meet the brain of Smiths.

She started joking that I was the guy who straightened the bullets for the chief engineer who could not shoot straight! She need not have done that.

It was one more validation of my guru's wisdom that we need to give up more to receive more.

Predictably, I was thrown into tougher assignments from them on. Like the China Lake algorithm project, developing ballistic models of weapons.

It was developed in the US navy's million-acre weapons development facility in California's Mojave Desert. It was called China Lake and the name got attached to the algorithm. This was a great opportunity for me to hone my skills in developing algorithms, mathematical modelling, and software development. One after another, I got involved in many programmes of importance for Smiths.

Oh, by the way, we the 'Tridev' had a great time travelling around the beautiful Cotswold area in which we lived. Our English friend Geoff took extra care to take us around, introducing us to the local culture and customs.

Our daughter was a small baby then, and it did not stop us from travelling to some historic places like Oxford, Warwick, and Stratford upon Avon or having a week-long trip to Paris. Our baby daughter was a great help to us—everyone let us get ahead in every conceivable queue!

After the successful completion of the secondment, we were transferred back to India and posted at our new avionics facility at Korwa. This place is about 100 miles south-east of Lucknow, with all the qualifications of small villages—dusty, isolated, terrible infrastructure, and poor people with golden hearts. We, the Tridev, were in for a rude shock as we reported to the general manager. He assigned us as system design managers in a department that did not officially exist.

The general manager was trying to go beyond just assembling systems and create design capability. He allocated a few of us as phantom resources with a hope of getting a design function approved by his board so that investments could flow in.

As the leader of a manufacturing facility, he was authorised to spend only for plant, equipment, buildings, and raw materials. He could not spend a dime on anything else; we were left with no moneys to develop any product in the phantom design department. After a purposeful stint in England, it hurt us bad to be back in India as phantom resources in a non-existent department.

We were to keep waiting till the corporate recognised us as a legitimate design function and open the money tap. So we waited. And waited. And waited. Nothing happened.

It was becoming clear that no one was in a mighty hurry to provide us with legitimacy. Our 'design department' became the butt end of the jokes in the township. It was determined by all that the boy who brought the tea twice a day was the busiest among us, and it was reasonably accurate.

It was bothering a few of us no end. What were we going to do? Keep waiting forever, or do something? We all wanted to get out of that isolated village which had no schools, colleges, hospitals, restaurants, or any entertainment. How could we market ourselves in the private sector and move to bigger cities, if we rot in a place without any significant achievements to show?

As I kept brooding, two words flashed in my mind—skunkworks. Lockheed Martin had created a way in which a small, well-funded, but loosely controlled team cut the bureaucracy and did radical development. This was aliased as skunkworks.

I had to do a skunkworks with a difference, without any funding! How does one spend money without having any money?

I sat down and asked myself, 'Why is money required in first place?' The answer was clear—to buy components that were needed to build the custom computer, hire engineers, and buy the software tools.

Supposing we were able scrounge around and find excess inventory of computer parts in the manufacturing facility? All the memory chips, processors, peripheral controllers and so on? The facility was manufacturing advanced avionics systems that were made of on-board computers, and since any government-owned enterprise was wasteful, it was bound to have overstocked items.

Bullseye!

And what would I do for the workforce needed? Why not convince the assembly line engineers to double down as software engineers for me after they finish their shift? They needed a polished resume as well to get into big cities!

Bullseye! Why not build three products, not just one? If we kept the hardware nearly the same but changed the software, they would be configurable products.

Hallelujah, all ducks in row!

Armed with this great idea, I set out to work on engineers in the assembly line and talked them into agreeing to put in the additional twenty hours a week to develop these products. This would be their passport to cities. Finding the components from the overstocked inventory took some persuasion. Managing other minor stuff was easy, and presto, we were ready for building the products—a navigation computer, a weapon-aiming computer, and a guidance computer.

We all recognised that each of us had to give up something we individually cherished to make this happen—our respective ego, individual ranks, evening revelry, weekends, and much sleep.

The whole team was excited at the prospect and worked hard for months to get the prototypes done. There was intense jubilation when they started working, and it was time to find a market for them. We needed someone to go out and sell them. But who?

After all, we were a government-run enterprise set up for manufacturing systems needed by the air force; government regulations and boundaries did not permit anything else. And in our misplaced enthusiasm, we had developed products for the army and the navy! Who was going to sell them?

It was left to me as the leader to deal with it. After all, I had created them without any understanding of the jurisdiction problems. I knew that it was a risky proposition, as this meant crossing some boundaries that were sacred. I just went ahead anyway to connect with army and naval headquarters to make presentations and give demos and very soon got back to our general manager with letters of intent worth millions of dollars.

We, the skunkworks team, were overjoyed. We had accomplished something unheard of, having developed not one, but three working prototypes without any budgetary support, and got LOIs worth millions! It sure felt like being in Lockheed Martin, if not in Apple. Sure enough, official letters started arriving at our GM's desk from the army and navy HQ, seeking appointments to discuss trials leading to bulk procurement.

I was summoned to meet him, and predictably, I walked into his room, head held high and chin up.

'You had no authority to meet customers and make commitments on our behalf,' yelled the general manager at me. It shocked me to the point I almost fell off from my chair. I was getting a dressing-down and was being accused of violating some archaic government rules, while I was expecting to be praised sky high. Who had ever created something out of nothing, like we had done? It just did not matter for the bureaucracy, and we were asked to shutter the projects down and wait for further instructions. After protracted discussions with the relevant government agencies, our general manager decided to transfer the know-how to agencies which won the production contract, once we backed out.

I was ordered to transfer the know-how to the appropriate organisation. It was really something we just could not take, to be the people to hand over all the design details, software listing, and prototypes to our competitors. We had to do go through those painful moments, and we felt like young mothers who were compelled by situations to put their newborn babies up for adoption.

That experience made a career decision for me; I decided to leave that organisation and join a private sector company, maybe a small one, which would be entrepreneurial and foster risk-taking and innovation.

As luck would have it, a small Indo-American company approached me with a job offer to be its global sales and marketing manager. It was a high-tech component manufacturing organisation, a start-up with young promoters at the helm. They wanted to move up the value chain, make electro-optics products, and were looking for a global sales head. They wanted someone who could not only talk well but who also understood technology; they were not selling soaps. Their clients were global brands in America, Europe, and Japan. I resigned my job and left for the coastal city of Pondicherry to join that start-up company.

The craziest thing was to be congratulated by the general manager for leaving his company. His send-off words? 'This is good for both of us and so wish you good luck!'

We had a grand send-off ceremony, and many of my friends and colleagues came out wishing us well. It was not easy for anyone to find a good job offer and leave from that place. The place had no telephones and no newspaper and was in total isolation. Getting a job like what I had got was considered as a great accomplishment. Some, though, felt I was being foolhardy to take the risk of joining a start-up.

It was clear in my mind that this was but a stepping stone for bigger things to go after, with other better jobs to come. All wondered what the magic formula was that helped me achieve this.

In my mind, it was plain and simple. I had taken the advice of the guru to heart and was willing to give up comfort, weekends, job security, etc. to get something that we all wanted.

And it worked!

TO WIN,
LEARN TO LET OTHERS WIN.

CHAPTER 4

❦

It's All Your Fault, Mr Immelt

The whole township had gathered on our front lawn to see us off, and it was heart-warming to see so many friends, colleagues, local shopkeepers, and servants gather. 'Did we recognise that we had so much of goodwill in this remote village in northern India?' I asked myself. I was very sure that at least *I* had not realised that. You get to know the value of what you are leaving behind only when you are leaving. We take it for granted while we have it, and this erodes the extrinsic value terribly.

We said the usual tearful farewells and made the customary promise to visit them back as soon as possible. We were leaving for Chennai, some 1,200 miles south, with very little reason for coming back, and yet we made that promise. All of us, me included, thought it was just a well-meaning remark, but events would play out to bring me back to that sleepy village in a couple of years. The love and affection of simple and honest people are more potent than anyone can imagine being.

That last day in that township was not without any drama either, a stark reminder for all of us how isolated and support-less the place was. It was perhaps a sharper reminder for those whom we were leaving behind, but it did not appear that they understood it. We were leaving the place anyways.

We kept waiting for the truck meant to transport our household goods, and it just did not show up at all. The township did not have a phone service in every house, and the mobile phones were not invented then. There was nothing we could do but keep waiting for the truck or try to arrange another truck somehow. Someone suggested we go the factory security and call the agent in Lucknow who took our commission.

We hurried and called the agent to find out what was going on and why the truck did not show up. After we called many times, someone answered the phone with a touch of irritation. It seemed like he had woken up from a slumber, and it showed. 'Sorry, sir, the truck we booked for you has not come from its previous run. It is yet to get back to Lucknow, and we don't know when it would show up. So there is nothing we can do. You can go ahead and fix some other truck if you want to.' With that curt response, the agent slammed the phone down.

Sorry? We were the ones feeling sorry, with all our goods packed, ready and lying in the yard. We had handed over the keys of the apartment and were ready to leave. We were in panic mode by now. What else could we do? We certainly could not cancel the travel and get back to the apartment.

Our friends did what all good friends do—they assured that they will find another truck and send the goods to our Chennai address and suggested we should simply leave. It was truly large-hearted of them, and we did not know what else we could do but consent. At that moment, something unbelievable happened. A truck rolled into the factory to deliver raw materials. Our friends accosted the driver and explained our difficult situation, and the driver readily agreed to transport our stuff to Chennai after unloading the goods at the factory. The goodwill of good people has uncanny ways of working, and we saw it play out then and there.

In what many of our friends considered as a divine twist, the truck driver's name was Raghavendra Singh; the first name being that of a famous seventeenth-century yogi. It was indeed miraculous to have a truck show up all of a sudden and help us out, and with a driver with a yogi's name. Life is never won without such selfless actions of friends and help from strangers. If we don't see divinity in such things, where else could we?

Having dodged the bullet, we set out to the railroad station. The train journey to Chennai would take nearly two days, and we had plenty of time to talk and think. My wife and I spent the time going through our five years in that remote village; we noted to our great satisfaction that we did enjoy the stay. We were particularly moved by the poor, simple, and honest people of the nearby villages. It was truly remarkable to see people happy and smiling, even though they were not assured of the next meal.

As the train kept chugging along, the reality of what I was venturing to do started to sink in slowly. It made me very anxious about our future. Here I was, getting paid for doing nearly nothing and providing well for my family with two small kids. And what did I do instead of just enjoying it all? I dashed it all by quitting the job, plunging into a start-up company, and taking on a role that I had never played before. And oh, by the way, the start-up company was serving a global market, which was very reluctant to buy anything from India. How would I succeed as global sales manager if the affluent G7 nations felt it was impossible to rely on India?

Several well-meaning friends in Korwa had tried their level best to persuade me to drop that plan and stay back, but I was adamant in moving on. They were very sure of my impending failure and started looking at us as if we were sacrificial goats. In their view, I was taking too much of a risky change, going from a software design role in a secure government-run enterprise to a start-up, private enterprise, trying to sell to reluctant clients in G7. It was triple trouble, according to many.

With nothing else to do in a moving train for two days, my mind took a dive into pessimism. 'Oh God, what have I done?' I started cursing myself as I kept looking at my wife and two small kids who were sleeping in the railcar. The thought that I might fail in the new job, putting them at risk, started eating me. The new company was struggling, making losses, and in debt—it was serving the tough American, European, and Japanese high-precision optical customers. While the company had exceptionally good equipment and skilled labour, clients felt that a country that could not pave smooth roads could hardly produce high-quality optical systems.

The company had its share of woes too; it was started by a very successful marketing wizard and, as is usual, his friends. They had no expertise in running complex organisations as none of them had operations expertise. The founder MD had a strategy to diversify into electro-optics systems that had better price point and profitability. He was looking for someone to execute a product strategy that would catapult them to success. It was me they chose.

'What if I failed miserably in the attempt?' The pressure was building in my mind and reached a breaking point. I could no longer keep it to myself and woke up my sleeping wife to share the concern.

'Why are you thinking of failing, rather than thinking of how you would succeed? Did you not succeed in an environment that was not even supportive or fostering success in Korwa? Why don't you draw lessons from that and apply?' asked my wife. She was proving once again that she was made of some serious and better stuff.

'I am not worried for myself,' I retorted. 'Rather about you and kids.' The egoistic husband had reared his head.

'You don't have to worry about us,' she continued. 'I will manage the household with any income you bring in, and you stay focused on succeeding.' With that said, she went back to sleep. Her words were very reassuring and encouraging, boosting my confidence.

The sacrifice she had made was not apparent to me then; it was not clear to me for a very long time. It would take me twenty years and another continent before it dawned on me. Many of us take our life partners for granted, and it is a terrible mistake.

Reassurance led to confidence, and it morphed into bravado. I took her advice too literally and was thinking how *I* had made it all a success so far. From that moment onwards it seemed that *I* was the secret behind all the success and it was *my* magic. This thought fuelled my ego as well, and by the time I joined the new company, my head was so heavy I could not even walk straight.

The environment in the new place did not help either. Being small and a start-up, people were over-aggressive; being lean, they demanded too much from each other; being underwater, there was no money for anything, which meant we had to be very innovative. Whoever found a way was a hero.

Armed with new-found enthusiasm and energy and an environment that encouraged a 'take no prisoners' attitude, I set upon to rewrite the history of that company. The founder managing director, Murali, encouraged and fuelled this approach as he was himself an aggressive person. He was kind of a marketing genius and had very clear understanding on how the human mind worked.

He personally mentored me and taught several aspects of brand creation, messaging, marketing, and negotiating among other things. In return, I worked hard in driving a sound product strategy. We worked like in a tango, and very soon we were on high gear with an expansion plan that called for releasing a product every year. The products would leverage the core competency of the company, which were high-tech optical systems. Built around that would be a complex web of electronics and software that added a very high value. This sure would fetch us higher price points and better profitability.

The young company had very bright engineering minds that had enormous appetite for hard work and innovation. These were great ingredients that helped successful execution of our product strategy. A mild-mannered Chief Technology Officer was a great pillar of strength, and we three became the engine of market growth—the CEO with his *strategic perspective,* the CTO with his *innovations and value engineering,* and me as CMO, the *'articulator' of the company brand.* All my old exploits and the skills I had picked up during my elocution contests and my duels with physicists started paying off.

I soon became the star spokesperson and brand ambassador for the company; I would be the final arbitrator on client messaging, after our marketing genius MD, of course!

The next three years were a great excitement for the company as we launched one product after another in quick succession to a resounding success. Thermal imaging camera and rigid endoscope and laser system hit the market with a bang, causing so much of splash. The company's fortune started looking brighter as the order book started swelling. The high-value-added products fetched very good margins, and our accountants were smiling more often. Our rapid growth ensured that we became the cynosure of all leading lights of that old French town.

This emboldened us no end, and we decided to participate in a global fair. After a detailed and careful evaluation we decided to participate in the MEDICA. This annual fair held in Dusseldorf, Germany, is considered to be the Mecca of high-tech medical industry. No other Indian company had participated in this prestigious trade fair so far, and we were excited that we would be creating history, in a way; the fair would fly the Indian flag on the grounds for the first time in its history.

'High-technology business is a highly networked business, and it is important to play in the same field as the clients. Participating in MEDICA will put our brand alongside some global brands in medical devices. That is big league,' urged Murali to the CFO, who was very reluctant to spend that kind of money. We could not fault that poor guy; he was seeing some good money in the company coffers after a long time. He was tired of managing finances at the edge of credit limits. Luckily, he yielded, and we started our prep.

We got busy with our advertising agency to design the stall, display units, marketing collaterals, videos, etc. We recognised that we were biting big by taking our brand to the Mecca of engineering. The precision engineering market was very conservative, dominated by countries like Germany, Japan, and Singapore which were well known for their discipline and hard work. We had to get the messaging very right, we thought.

Somehow, the advertising agency was having difficulty in getting that point. Here we were, trying to project ourselves as a solid, conservative, technology company having a world-class manufacturing facility, and they were coming out with themes like thieves breaking into our facility and trying to steal our best-in-class equipment rather very unsuccessfully! They were perhaps too much used to consumer goods clients and were going for a cinematic content. We were getting very frustrated at this.

I decided to take matters into my hands and create my own script. With that thick folder in my hand, I approached Murali. 'Here is how the video should present our capabilities. To make it clear, I have it written down scene by scene, defining the backdrop, music (Mozart), dialogue, and so on. Why don't you have a look'? He was a bit puzzled and was not expecting this from me. 'How can this first-time marketing guy do better than the ad agency?' he must have thought. He took the folder nevertheless and promised to give a read in the night.

He was all smiles and full of excitement when he came to work the next day. 'This is unbelievable work! Kudos to you! This is exactly what I had in mind and what we need to emphasise. You really surprised me, a pleasant one. Here is the deal. You take charge of the entire video shoot. You will approve every shot, every sound, every word, and you need not even check with me.' That he meant every word he said and it was not mere encouragement became clear when he instructed the ad agency to go strictly by what I would say.

From that moment, I was *directing the director* who was filming the shoot. The poor fellow had to get a sign off from me for every shot he composed. It was a marvellous experience for me though, directing a fifteen-minute video that was to be shown at an international fair. Maybe I should have gotten a telly award if not an Oscar for a debutant director!

The greatest satisfaction for me in the whole deal was the way *Murali let me handle the whole thing*. He could have dismissed me off when I made the proposal; he was the expert in marketing and branding while I was just a novice from a government enterprise, and yet he let me go and win. This episode taught me a lesson: *To win, let others win.* He demonstrated the wisdom of harnessing the power of others in a team and letting them win. He stepped back and let me tap into my creativity, and sure enough, we had a classic video that was worthy of being shown in market like Europe.

At that very moment, my head and ego, which were so swollen all along, shrank down to the right size. *How could I think I was the one winning, the raison d'être all along?* How stupid I had become in thinking that way. I won in Korwa by harnessing the hard work and sacrifice of young engineers who teamed up with me as skunkworks. It was not *me* but *we* who had won. This was what my wife was pointing out in that moving train as we journeyed from Korwa, and it took so long for me to really understand.

The excitement over the MEDICA trip got doubled as we decided to combine this with another business development trip. As the travel itinerary evolved, I realised that *it would take us literally around the world!* We were scheduled to start from Pondicherry, travel all over Europe, America, Japan, Singapore, and head back. We would be truly going around the world in forty-one days! We would become the modern Magellans.

We decided to split the world between us and meet as many clients and prospects as we could.Murali would largely focus on existing clients, and I would focus on the prospects. It made enormous sense for him to leverage existing relationship that he had built over years, and for me it did not matter either way; as a newcomer, I had no relationship with anyone.

The preparation for the world tour was in full swing: getting the display models, samples, boards, collaterals, and CDs; the list of things to do grew forever without any end. We were on a shoestring budget and would not be able to hire expensive labour in Dusseldorf. We had the vendors make the exhibits cleverly, in modular *push-to-fit form*, so that just the two of us could assemble and erect all the display units.

When you have a founder CEO as your teammate, 'two equals one' *is the new math that works*. He was gracious enough to offer the support in all physical labour, but I did not want to take that offer. So I just kept an eye on this 'push-to-assemble' principle before approving any displays. Finally, everything was done and ready to go.

With all fanfare we shipped the material and boarded our flight to Germany. It was all excitement during the flight, and it felt as if we were going to conquer Germany, as if we were Porus attacking Europe. We hit the ground as soon as we landed and got busy meeting clients. Feeling wonderful, we showed up at the fairground at Dusseldorf and met the fair coordinator to get to know our booth allocation.

We had little inkling about the disaster waiting to happen. We did not have to wait long for it. Within minutes of our greeting her, the coordinator informed us that the fair director had rescinded our participation permit and we just could not participate. She would not elaborate on that but advised us to meet the director immediately and plead with him. She was obviously feeling bad to see us come from a poor country, so far away, and be told that we had to simply go back without participating.

We hurried to meet the director only to find that the problem appeared to be bigger than what we thought. He talked slowly, deliberately, and systematically, like all Germans do. He had not been consulted before our registration was accepted. He stated apologetically, 'Dear Herren, our MEDICA fair is a prestigious one occurring every year in which *only* globally famous brand companies participate. We are very careful in letting companies participate, as we don't want our brand name affected by any new company putting up a poor show. New and small companies don't have the understanding or the money to prepare well. You are an obscure little company from India, and how can we allow you to sully the fair's brand?'

'We may be small but are well known in the high-tech optical systems industry. If you want, we can arrange reference calls with leading German brands right now,' protested my CEO. It did not help much.

While he was willing to encourage new and upcoming companies like ours, he could not take risk in letting *us* participate, as he knew very little of us personally. Our protests did not carry us very far. 'I just don't have the luxury of sparing time now to evaluate you or talk to the references you provide. At any rate, the rules of the fair clearly state that participation decision is entirely mine, and I am within my powers to revoke it at any time without any reason.'

With that, he dismissed us and added, what was in his mind, a friendly advice, 'I suggest you don't even unpack the boxes but take them back and leave. This will save any expense you may incur by engaging local labour.' He obviously knew that we could not afford that expense, and it was better that way.

This was totally unexpected, and it took a while to recover and respond to him. Any amount of pleading or arguing did not help. He just did not want to risk the reputation of the fair by allowing a nondescript, young company from India to participate.

There was nothing much we could do but agree with him, and having come this far, we did not want to give up either. After discussing amongst ourselves, we made an offer that was within his direction and yet gave us a tiny opening. 'It is still Friday, and the fair will open for public viewing only from Monday. What if we set up our stall, invite you to personally evaluate our exhibits and then take a final decision? The risk is ours, and we will go by your final call.' Murali was at his negotiating best.

We had the whole weekend in front of us before the fair opened, so he would not lose anything; if at all, we would be the losers if he eventually decided to ask us to leave. This appeared very logical and reasonable to the German mind, and he agreed. 'I still reserve the right to refuse after seeing the set-up. As long as you will be able to disassemble and take everything away by Sunday evening, if I refuse, I am OK with this.'

We assured him that we could do that and got his reluctant nod. What was supposed to help us assemble the set-up quickly would now help us to disassemble it quickly, and that was going to save our chances.

With a heavy heart, we set out to erect our stall, all by ourselves. Putting up large art panels, focus lamps, decorative pieces, the large TV, etc. were easy to do. But what about the 'corner cube'?

The 'corner cube' was in fact a tall cuboid, a 4 feet ´ 4 feet ´ 8 feet glass case in which high-precision optical components were to be arranged in an artistic way. It had an appearance of water flowing down a rock structure with velvet cloth draped on a set of pillars with varying heights. The optical components were coated with multilayered anti-reflection coating that changed colour as you walked around the display. Our engineers cleverly made use of the diffraction properties of optical coatings.

The glass cube had a small 3 ′ 3 cut-out at the bottom with a sliding door through which one had to get in, arrange the components, and get out. I was the 'chosen one' to get in and arrange the displays. I slipped into this glass cage with all the pillars, velvet cloth, and optical components, much to the amusement of the folks setting up the neighbouring stalls. 'We would love to see how you *get out* after arranging the display, without knocking them down' was the chorus.

With the scepticism of the onlookers, time pressure, and the German Damocles's sword hanging above our head, I started the arrangement with single-minded focus. Slowly, everything else disappeared from my mind. I could not see the stall, the neighbours, my boss, or the noisy forklifts that were moving around to set up some large displays in other stalls. I could only see the components that needed to be arranged in an artistic way. With enormous patience and concentration, I finished the task in about three hours.

A burst of clapping broke my spell, and I could now hear a chorus saying, 'We love it.' I looked up to see a small crowd of people watching with great appreciation the colourful arrangement. The optical components were truly shining with a dazzle of colours as the people moved around. It was truly impressive.

'Let us see how you are able to come out through the small door without knocking things down,' said the curious onlookers. Some of them took out their video cameras to capture the scene that was to unfold. This was an occasion which, whether it was a successful or a failed attempt, it deserved to be captured on camera. I was sitting in a squat-like position, the lotus posture of a yogi; I unlocked my legs, bent sideways, and slithered like a snake and gently slid out, leaving the exhibits intact. I got out to the rapturous clapping of the crowd.

'You guys are in. I am delighted to let you participate,' boomed a voice. Neither Murali nor I had noticed that the director of the fair was *among* the onlookers. We did not know when he had come to inspect our booth. He was very pleased at what we had done, and the crowd's enthusiastic support was an additional endorsement. He was only too glad to approve our participation immediately. It was such a big relief.

Where was Murali when all these things were going on? He was just sitting in a corner, letting me do the deed and bask in the limelight. He did not interfere even for a moment, nor did he harass me with instructions. He just stepped back and let me do it.

He won by letting me win.

All the stress, tiredness, and jet lag suddenly hit us, and we both were only too happy to skip our dinner and hit the bed. We slept like logs. It was a moment of pride of creating history as Indian national flag was hoisted at the grand opening on Monday.

We were literally getting mobbed by visitors. Every OEM in the medical devices market was represented at the fair, and they were very surprised to see the high quality of the components we had displayed. They were making a beeline to visit our booth and get to know more about our capability. Our customers from Europe and the United States were there, and they felt very proud of us and of themselves too. They earned that right, having been the pioneers in discovering and developing us in India.

As it happens at all fairs, visitors came in bursts. There were short gaps when no one visited us. We both just sat in a corner, listening to the baritone German voice of the video playing in an unending loop. We were just soaking in the exultation and started conversing on how to leverage all the interest this had generated. 'My concern is around our production capacity and capability. It is wonderful to have a bulging order book, but it could end up as a horror if we are not able to deliver on time,' said Murali.

Maybe I got carried away by all the adulation that was flowing towards me. I got bold and told him, 'In my view we don't have the management capability to tackle a big order book. From what I have been seeing, neither you nor the COO knows anything about operations. I, on the other hand, can help if you want me to.' If he got offended, he did not show it. He just asked me, sarcastically perhaps, how long I would take to show some improvements if he gave the job to me.

I snapped back, 'I would turn the company performance around in a year.'

He was obviously and rightly upset at my bravado. He responded sharply, 'I would be happy if you could show some *noticeable improvement* in a couple of years. You have no idea of our manufacturing process, and you did not show any inclination to learn either.'

Recognising that I had touched a raw nerve, I dropped the subject altogether and treated it closed.

Little did I anticipate that he would keep this conversation in mind for more than a month and act on it. When it happened, my life changed forever, *again*.

Once we wrapped up the successful fair, we went our ways, travelling to meet our clients in different countries in Europe. He covered our existing clients in mainland Europe while I was scheduled to meet our clients and develop new prospects in the United Kingdom. This travel took me to England, Wales, and Scotland. We were to meet in London and travel to the United States together.

The travel in the United Kingdom was largely eventless, meeting clients and prospects to pitch our story. Well, almost eventless. There were a couple of incidents that made a deep impact on me. They were the 'fax to nowhere' and 'Only Irish Paddy' incidents.

The 'fax to nowhere' was personally a disappointing story. At one of the meetings, the entire management had assembled to listen to my talk about our capabilities and see the video clip showcasing our capabilities and equipments. They were very impressed by what they saw. Their managing director was keen on working with us and so he directed the reluctant buyer to try us out with a sample order.

The buyer was reluctant for a very valid reason. He felt that the communication infrastructure in India was not good enough, and it would put an unreasonable burden on him in doing business with us. But their managing director kept insisting that he should try us out; under duress, he agreed to try us out. There was a condition, though. 'Paddy, I will try to fax the order three times,' he said. 'If the fax goes successfully, the order will be yours, and if it does not, you will have to come back ten years later.' He kept his word and tried three times, but the fax just did not go through. I was shown the door with a return permit valid after ten years! This was the difficulty many entrepreneurs faced in India those days. They had to succeed in spite of the governments.

The other story was more unpleasant, almost nasty, bordering on racism. I showed up for a meeting with the managing director of a small company. He appeared a bit confused to see me as I was ushered into his office. 'Are you the Paddy I am scheduled to meet?' he asked incredulously. He was perhaps expecting to meet a tall, fair, blue-eyed Irishman and in walked a brown fellow from India. He promptly called the security to escort me out, muttering that he had agreed for the meeting only because my name was given as Paddy, an Irish name. I was led out into a cold, snowy day, and they did not even bother to hail a taxicab for me. I just took it in my stride and chose to remember the vast majority of the British who had been so helpful and had showered affection and love.

After finishing other meetings with prospects, I rejoined my boss at London. 'We need to quickly close our partnership agreement with the "endoscope" guys,' he said when we connected back. 'Those guys were very excited when they visited our booth in Dusseldorf. We have a great manufacturing skill, they have a simple design, and this synergy should get a good quality endoscope at affordable price in this market,' he continued.

It was typical of Murali to think strategically around market segmentation all the time. 'We should know whom we are serving' was his common refrain.

The 'endoscope' guys were more eager than us, and this helped close the deal quickly. They did the preliminary design and had a good network in the market. They agreed to come down to our works in India and work a few weeks to transfer the design know-how.

Our sense of achievement and confidence were boosted, and we felt vindicated at the participation in the expensive global expo. We sure would have felt awkward meeting our CFO had we gone back empty-handed. CFOs generally love collecting money more than spending money, and ours was no exception.

With that agreement signed up, we departed for America. We were hoping to repeat the 'endoscope experience' in America by signing a similar know-how agreement for the thermal cameras. The very thought of making thermal cameras triggered memories of the hard and long battle we had fought to win that contract from our client in India. The transatlantic flight to America was a long flight, and we had all the time to recollect those past events. We had designed a thermal imaging camera around that American company's detector. The specialty of this hand-held camera was its ability to cut through dense smoke and show a clear picture of what lay ahead. This was particularly useful in firefighting applications. The data showed that more people usually died due to lack of oxygen than actual fire. And it was impossible to locate those who were down asphyxiated as the dense smoke obscured the vision. We had set out to change all that.

'How did you prove to the testing guy that he was seeing when he kept saying he could not?' asked Murali. We had gone through this story several times, but it was interesting to talk about it often.

Those trials were literally back-breaking. Wearing a heavy firefighter suit, breathing tank strapped on my back, and wearing a chunky face mask, I had gotten into the smoke chamber. My job was to train the customer's agent who would be doing a complete testing. The smoke chamber was very soon engulfed in dense diesel fumes, and we had to locate a dummy lying somewhere on the ship's deck, simulating a fainted sailor. While I was able to see through clearly, the agent insisted that he could not. This went on for quite some time, till I decided to shock him by shouting that he was stepping on something and he was about trip and fall. Instinctively, he replied that the dummy was at least ten feet away, and then he had to admit that the camera was working well.

Murali was referring to that crazy incident. We laughed at that experience and looked forward to closing the production deal with the sensor company.

With the progress we were making in another project—our engineers were developing a thin film reflector-based head up display—we both felt we were on cloud nine. The fact that we were literally on the top of the clouds was not lost on us, and we thoroughly enjoyed the situation.

We started our business meetings as soon as we landed in Washington DC. We were exploring the possibility of selling our night vision goggles to Uncle Sam. It was a tough sell, and we did not make any headway without any local partner pitching for us. DC was indeed a complex puzzle that we could not understand.

Our next stop was New Mexico to close a partnership agreement with the thermal camera sensor company. The relatively small connecting plane landed in Albuquerque, a leisurely place where everyone had enough time to be nice to each other. There could not be any other place contrasting more with Washington, DC. The CEO of the company was there, waiting to receive us. He was a tall Texan, all dressed in style in a cowboy hat and long boots, and he was given to backslapping. It took a while for us to understand his drawl. He took us around his facility and proudly explained their entire product line. We almost disappeared in what appeared to be very large sofa as we moved to his office for negotiating the contract. Pleasantries over, the hard bargaining started. He negotiated very hard, and we were worried he would lasso us, if not draw his guns and shoot. 'I like to work with you fellas' his voice boomed. 'And I do want to partner with you. But you got to get it that your are dependent on me more than I am on you. The royalty you are willing to pay simply won't cut, fellas. You got to do better than this. Let me take you out for lunch, and you guys can munch over better terms to offer there.'

He took us to a nearby steak house, which treated us like a visiting royalty. There was a small music band standing around our table, wearing very, very large Mexican hats, playing violin, and singing Spanish songs. What did we get to eat? As strict vegetarians, we ended up eating a large potato. One large potato! The only thing we could munch on was the contract terms.

As I watched Murali carry forward the negotiations, my heart moved in a lump and clogged my throat. It was very comical to note the change in our moods and stance once we got back to the negotiating table. All the music and frolic evaporated in the New Mexico heat, and we became very sombre again.

'In any partnership, we always have equal dependency,' started Murali. 'To assume that any one has more dependency is a bad start. While it is indeed true that our prototype was based on your sensor, it will not take very long for us to change our design. Our computer hardware and software is flexible enough to adapt to another sensor. What I am looking for is a clear win-win,' he concluded.

It was very clear that we were losing the argument and negotiations were breaking down. The Texan was in no mood to acquiesce, and my boss was in no hurry to yield. I was getting all tensed up; after all, we had won a multimillion-dollar-contract based on the prototype based on their detector, and production agreements were breaking down. My boss was talking about changing the design. I was not at all keen to get into the smoke chamber again to prove to someone who would claim he was not able to see through the device, that he was actually seeing!

The Texan abruptly got up and wished us the entire best and safe voyage back home. We reached our hotel in the evening with no agreement closed. We were to leave the town next day. I was feeling pretty bad and started making some fervent pleas with Murali to yield and close the deal before we left.

He just smiled and said, '*We should be willing to lose if we are keen on winning.*' I just did not get it; we were not winning, were we?

We went about having our dinner as if we were tourists. As we were about to retire to bed, the Texan called. In his typical drawl, he offered to give us some more concessions if we were willing to relax some demands. He just did not want us to go back to other end of the world empty-handed. "We in South don't send our guests with an empty stomach,' he growled. My boss agreed to yield on the conditions they felt thorny, and we were back in the game.

The rest of the things moved very fast; we woke up early in the morning, packed, and drove to the company, and there was celebration. We signed the agreement, had the usual photo session, and left. It all closed so quickly that the prolonged negotiations seemed like a dream. San Francisco was waiting. My boss's guidance prevailed; *we were willing to lose the deal, and so we won.* It was a new learning that I would be putting to good use in the near future.

San Francisco kept us very busy, and we were not spared even at the airport. It was pouring heavily and there were flood warnings, none of which deterred the folks who wanted to come and meet my boss. By the time we finished our meetings there, I was close to being a nervous wreck. Travelling with a founder managing director for a month was not exactly all that fun. The stress was showing!

His response? He was all grace himself. He instructed the ticket agent at the check-in counter to seat us in different rows in the long-haul flight to Singapore via Hong Kong! The air hostesses were more confused as to why coming from same company we were sitting away from each other. It was truly very nice of him, but it helped me relax, watch some meaningless movies, and sleep.

It was all meeting clients in Singapore, the city country that never ceases to inspire. The whole environment was one of hardworking people, and work got done at lightning speed. It was travelling back home thereafter!

We finally reached home after circumnavigating the world in forty-one days! It felt truly like being a Magellan; we were rather luckier than him as we reached home alive, while Magellan did not!

I was busy preparing the tour report and regaling my other colleagues with funny stories for a couple of weeks. It was the calm before the storm. This frolic was abruptly cut short one day when Murali called me into his office for a one-on-one meeting.

He threw his charming smile and said, 'It is time to get back to work and face up the challenge you accepted. I am now transferring you as head of operations, and you will manage the entire factory too. And don't forget the turnaround you promised in Dusseldorf.' He was calling me out on my claim.

'You judged that we did not know how to manage operations well and claimed that you could do a better job. Maybe you are right. So I am now giving you an opportunity to prove yourself,' he said, and continued, 'For my part, even if you show marginal improvement in a couple of years, I will let you continue.' He probably ignored my claim about faster turnaround for my own benefit. Nor was he specific on what he would do if I failed. It was perhaps implied that I would have to go.

With mixed feelings, I drove down to the factory, about ten miles away from the corporate office. The incumbent COO welcomed me with customary politeness; the shop manager presented a bouquet and conducted me around. This was followed by a meeting with the union leader and a detailed status briefing by the COO.

The outgoing COO was one of the founding members of the company, well respected and liked for his friendly style. He was very involved with the workers, and he knew the intricacies of the manufacturing process first-hand. He was a bit shocked that I was being sent over for the turnaround and for a valid reason. All along, I had been focused on diversifying the company into electro-optics products and had not shown any inclination to learn the high-precision optics manufacturing process. I was out and out a product sales leader, and now I was being tasked with a turnaround that had eluded us for years.

He wished me well, shook hands with me, and left for the corporate office—to take over the job I had relinquished. Murali had done a role switch.

As I sat in my cabin and watched the factory shop floor through the transparent plastic wall, I could clearly sense that all the eyes were on me, even though no one was actually looking at me. Each one was perhaps thinking what I was thinking: 'What is the different thing I am going to do to succeed when the others with so much of personal involvement struggled with?'

They kept observing me, and I kept thinking about the way forward. After several days of observing and scores of review meetings, I stumbled on the answer. No, it was not some grand point that emerged out of the reviews; it was not even discovered on that high-tech shop floor.

It was a bolt from the past. It was something I had learnt observing Murali at the expo at Dusseldorf. *He had let me win, thereby winning himself. The same way he let me win during the video shoot.*

It was a strange feeling; the entire sequence seemed to have been reversed! I had gotten the answer first in Germany for a question that I would ask myself a month later in India! Our minds have a strange way of connecting dots, if we let it.

Yes, it was becoming clearer, as viewed from this perspective, why my predecessor had difficulties. He would get personally involved in the minutest detail of every aspect of the manufacturing process, while perhaps not so much on what he, *and he alone*, could have provided—*a* visionary *leadership*. He was not letting others win by persistently trying to win it for them. In that process he lost as well.

In two ways I was different. One, being an electronics engineer who had quarrelled with chemistry, I had no appetite for optics manufacturing process. Two, my expertise was building a high-calibre team and holding them accountable for delivering on a powerful, shared vision.

Yes, the surest way of winning was to let the team just go and win. Win what? That is where I would step in by clearly *defining what a win would be—something they had never anticipated.* I kept thinking about this, and the game plan slowly emerged in my mid. I was now dealing with shop floor workers, who were millers, turners, fitters, grinders, polishers, optics coaters, and assemblers and not the qualified software engineers who had made a splash with me on the skunkworks programme.

I thought, 'I will have to craft a vision that was down-to-earth, catchy, and exciting, and one that could be understood and embraced by this unionised labour. A sort of a mantra for prosperity, yes, it will have to address their aspirations of prosperity with financial incentives.' It would address productivity increase along with prosperity increase. This made more sense; *prosperity through productivity* would surely be a catchy slogan. Since I had promised a dramatic turnaround to my managing director, this would have to be truly a remarkable thing that should have his head shaking in disbelief. I knew it by now.

'Six, twelve, twenty,' I told him, when I presented my new vision, and his head *did* shake in disbelief.

'What?' he exclaimed. 'Are you committing to grow our revenue by six, twelve, and twenty times the baseline value over the next three years?'

I just nodded.

'You must be crazy,' he concluded.

'Do you want it or not?' I persisted.

Of course he wanted that, but he was not sure if he should buy that or walk away. This kind of growth was something he was not anticipating and so could not refuse it. 'But how is he going to do it and with what magic?' he must have thought.

What he perhaps did not recognise was that his words about letting others win were more potent for me than he meant them to be. The meanings of words deepen based on individual experience, and what is accomplished depends on the context. Whoever is in control of a context gets a chance to redefine the meaning.

So for me, 'letting others win if we want to win' was a mantra that was so potent. I went to work the team with that. Having defined what the win was with 'six, twelve, twenty' mantra, I started working on defining what the word 'others' meant. The 'others' needed to include each and every function that was part of the complex operations and manufacturing chain. We laboured hard to streamline the org structure, brought in professional functional managers, established an IT function, and beefed up production planning and control. We optimised the workflow; implemented a production management system; and introduced design automation, assembly line automation, and Toyota production system elements.

And I did what I liked to do the most; I spent hours walking the shop floors, exciting the teams, writing energising stories of our successes, giving public recognition to employees—in short, anything that could kick up the motivation level of our employees. The labour union was on my side as they liked the slogan Prosperity through Productivity and they sure appreciated that we did not word it as Productivity for Prosperity.

When the first year rolled out and the books were tallied, we saw, much to our delight, that *we had delivered revenue nearly six times the previous year!* The mantra 'six, twelve, twenty' was working!

There was all-round jubilation in the company, and we were rewarded by the board with great incentives and a 'rolling shield' for outstanding performance. We repeated this turnaround the next year and delivered revenue that was ten times the base revenue, close enough for the 'twelve' part of the mantra. More jubilation and celebrations followed, and soon enough, we were getting noticed by all, including bankers, local politicians, and government agencies. We were becoming the talk of the town, literally!

This was a clear and one more vindication of the lesson: *if you want to win let others win.* I had formed an 'A Team' and let them loose, stepped back, provided an exciting vision, energised them, enabled them, and set high expectation. I called it the '4E model' of transforming a team, the four Es being Envision, Enable, Energise, and Expect. It worked like magic.

As we were preparing ourselves for the third-year growth towards 'twenty' times the base year, dark clouds started gathering around us. An eye-catching success does what it implies—catches the attention of all sorts of people. Many of them turned out to be unfriendly towards us. This led to some scary situations that we did not anticipate and called for skills we never had—*circus skills and transmigration skills.*

Our security products division was making night vision devices for defence and police departments. When Federal Intelligence wanted to buy from us, we were overjoyed and thought this was one more chance to diversify our market. Little did we realise that they were, in fact, satisfying themselves based on some murmur that our security procedure was up to the mark. The Intelligence Bureau thought that the best way to test our procedures was to buy a few pieces and come down for user acceptance trials. This would get them into our facility and give them an opportunity to check every aspect of the manufacture and sale.

When two of their agents showed up at our factory, we were ready for them and demonstrated our strict security procedures by subjecting them to its rigour. When we thought all was going well, they surprised us by demanding that we do a night trial on a fishing boat, deep into the sea. The night vision devices help to see in the dead of the night—the period after the sun has set but the moon is yet to rise. Generally, these trials are done on land. While the request was unusual, it had to be complied with.

We hired a catamaran from a local fisherman and set out into deep sea. Once into the sea, we had to stand up on the bobbing catamaran and conduct the trial. This turned out to be trickier than we had anticipated or were prepared for. Just imagine trying to stand firm on a catamaran bobbing on the restless sea, without even a life vest to save you if the boat capsizes!

The other episode was even trickier. We had to get into others' heads and 'see what they were seeing'—in fact, *what others claimed they were not able to see.* We were conducting the night trials at an abandoned airstrip, and the customer representative who was testing the products kept insisting that he was not able to see anything. Every time he said that, I borrowed the device from him to check and invariably found that it *was* working. This happened a few times to my puzzlement before he burst into laughter, asking me to calm down. He was just kidding.

For me it was an unsolvable problem; I wondered, 'How can I prove someone wrong when he claims he is unable to see? Only by transmigrating into his body?'

Time and again the principle of 'letting others to win if you want to win' was tested, and every time it worked like magic. When you assume a leadership position, your primary responsibility is to let others succeed. Many a times, leaders err in assuming that they are the solution for the problems and end up as the cause for accentuating the problems.

Complex organisations and markets demand a wide variety of skills, and it is irrational for anyone to believe that they possess all those skills.

Even if a leader has a wide repository of skills, he/she may not have all the time needed to solve all problems. This is so simple to understand that it gets overlooked often. Sometimes, ego takes over, distorting the rational thought process. Sometimes, leaders get pressured into believing that the teams expect them to know everything and do stupid things.

These were just skirmishes, and we had no clue that a 'Moby Dick' was about to ram into our boat. When it hit us, everything would be thrown overboard and we would shake violently. This was building up gradually without anyone of us having inkling.

It was the third year of our rapid-growth phase, the 'twenty' part of the mantra—twenty times the revenue just two years back. The machines were spinning wildly, inventories flowed, and all the pneumatic hand drills hummed. The thin film coating materials sputtered non-stop, and we even introduced a third shift. The throughput rate was building up nicely. The production planning and control system developed by the young IT team was chugging along fine.

All of our clients were feeling happy with these improvements, except some government clients— somehow they seemed to be displeased at our growth and started throwing roadblocks on our path to growth. The way the shipments worked was that we would get a consignment ready and have it inspected by a resident inspector, who would check the consignment to his heart's content and affix a QA seal on it; he would also sign off on the shipment documents. These signed documents and proof of dispatch were needed to get our payments authorised.

The resident inspector was *actually* residing in the factory and hence had all the opportunity and responsibility to inspect whatever he could lay his eyes on—raw materials, assembly process, finished goods, or surface treatment. This gave him an opportunity to delay the process whenever he pleased or stop it outright whenever he was displeased.

He started small, raising procedural objections, and very soon, he started walking around the shop floor, raising red flags on the process, which was beyond his purview. He started holding consignments from being dispatched over trivial matters. He went to the extent of raising questions on our JIT (just in time) inventory management practices.

'You are not running a JIT but a JAT (just after time),' he commented sarcastically several times, although he was hardly qualified in the tricky science of inventory management.

Slowly, finished goods inventory started piling up on the shop floor, while our factory was cranking production at breakneck speed. This was disastrous for our profitability as the cost of carrying inventory was very high. Banks began to notice that we were behind on shipment more often and we were sailing very close to the limits.

This started stressing all of us, and very soon it led to a breaking point. We could not stop the assembly line without risking missing the annual goals, and we kept producing until the break point was reached. We just had to stop the line as we ran out of raw materials; the 'pull' system meant that we could only pull more inventory if the finished goods left the factory. The intense pressure and frustration at not being able to do anything about it was making it difficult to operate. The tension was palpable, and everyone lost out in the bargain. The interpersonal relationship amongst us senior executives began to strain.

As I kept wondering how to get out the situation, one of my friends called me from Bangalore. He was a VP at the global software development centre of GE Medical systems, and he wanted to check if I was interested in becoming a six sigma Master Black Belt—MBB as it was called.

'MBB? Never heard of it,' I said. He insisted I should try it, and so I decided to give it a try. So I did.

The job interview was done like an assembly line with the VP, CEO, and HR manager, and the president seeing me one after another on the same day. It started in the morning at 9 a.m., and by 5 p.m., I had the GE job offer on hand. At GE, when they said that 'speed was a part of their value system', they meant it.

I was very curious to know why I was selected; after all I had no idea about what six sigma was all about. The job interview conversation was all around what I had done so far. 'In the GE world, quality champions need to come with business experience. They could not be bureaucrats from Inspection. We know about the transformation you did in that optics company, and that is exactly what we are looking for,' explained 'DAP' or D. A. Prasanna. He was the president and managing director of GE Medical Systems South Asia. He continued to elaborate, 'Jack Welch has launched a global initiative for implementing six sigma transformation, and we are hiring you to lead it for us in India. We have three manufacturing companies and a software unit, and you will be the leader for all the units.'

The offer was very lucrative in many different ways and impossible to refuse. The money was good, and who would not love to participate in an initiative launched by the legendary Jack Welch? He was shaking up the entire global corporate world. With jubilation I went back to Pondicherry.

Murali was taken aback when I tendered my resignation. He tried to persuade me to stay on, but my mind was made up. With much reluctance, he agreed to let me go, and it was very painful for me too. He respected me so much, had mentored me so much and had challenged me so much. Above all this, he had given me the space to experiment with my ideas of organisational transformation. He was humble enough to stand aside and let me win. He would remain in my mind forever as a mentor who helped me to realise who I was.

Time and tide wait for none, and so it took me to the demanding but exciting world of GE. I started my GE life as a six sigma Champion. 'Your performance goal is to deliver up to 0.5 per cent increase in operating margin through various six sigma projects,' said DAP as he welcomed me into his fold. I wondered about that—how many quality champions carried a *financial* goal? This meant the quality champion had to know how the business was run, not some rule book.

The 'Champion' had to deliver the results by identifying 'money eaters' in the company, build a team around that corner, and *make them* plug the money loss. Again, the mantra 'letting others win' reared its head, if I wanted to win as a six sigma Champion. It was never about the Champion rolling up the sleeves and getting dirty or acting 'Yoda' and delivering simple words with complex interpretations. *The Champion had to let and facilitate the six sigma teams to win.*

The way GE went about achieving quality improvements through six sigma was very interesting. It used complex and advanced statistical tools to determine how well that particular set of work instructions was performing. Mathematics revealed the areas where improvement was needed, and then the problem was fixed by changing the work instructions or a particular design. After the changes were made, the new instructions were executed, and the results were collected and analysed to see if the new process improvement was *statistically significant.* This was because any improvement could have been a random chance occurrence not caused by the changes made.

Clearly, this involved two things. One, identifying the areas that were costing lots of money for the company—called as big Y hurt areas. Second, convincing the senior leaders of those areas to let the best persons in those areas work full time to work on improvement projects. This was always the most difficult part, as the best persons were always kept busy doing the work rather than allowing them to work on some improvement projects.

Six sigma projects were done full-time, with plenty of classroom training in complex statistical tools, workflow, data collection, analysis, and correction, and then prove out. The employees who led the improvement projects were called Black Belts. It was the responsibility of the Champion to push the leadership team to make that investment and ensure that the Black Belts succeeded. The Champion's success was measured by the success of the Black Belts.

It was obviously a difficult thing to accomplish. In almost all the companies, leadership teams invariably believe that they have a clear idea of the problem areas, but they are rarely able to pinpoint what exactly is going wrong—the 'root cause'. But they start acting like experts and believe they know what the root causes are, and hence know how to fix the problem. It is generally glorified as the 'managerial gut feeling' and sometimes celebrated as a 'Moses' call. More often than not, a statistical analysis on the actual data shows that the root cause is very different, surprising the managers. This is because what the gut feeling tells the managers is a *conclusion about the past,* while a corrective action calls for a *prediction about the future.*

Herein lies the organisational dilemma. They depend on the managerial gut feeling for faster decision-making as many times they just cannot wait to collect all the data. Recognising the difference between *decisions about future* and *conclusions about the past* does not come easy, as one feeds into other.

This onerous task of helping managers dismantle their beliefs lies on the six sigma Champion. The Champion is expected to adopt *any which means* to get this accomplished, and I was pretty good at that. In one extreme case, when one of our suppliers refused to accept the recommendation of my Black Belt, I sat in front of the president of that company and refused to leave until he agreed to launch the improvement plan of my Black Belt!

Over the next two years, I was all over the organisation, driving improvement in manufacturing, sales, marketing, logistics, inventory, and software development. We went to all the key suppliers and demanded they do six sigma improvement projects. We helped train their folks in that and shared the gains achieved. My Japanese six sigma guru and I had the rare opportunity of training the entire board of directors of our multi-billion-dollar joint-venture partner in six sigma. It was a rare kind of experience teaching complex statistical tools to the greying and balding executive members of the board. But they were equally enthusiastic in learning the new tricks as it were. Whoever said that one could not teach a new trick to an old horse had not seen those board executives.

As we kept launching these projects, we could see the quality improvement sweep across the GE unit, suppliers, and joint venture partners. As a recognition and reward for the success, I was promoted as head of the manufacturing facility. This was also a part of the grand design of six sigma programmes. Go-getters became six sigma Champions, delivered great results, and moved back into a business role.

Jack Welch moved the global six sigma programme to the next level by declaring that the 'projects' phase was over and six sigma was the only 'way we work'. Our president, DAP, felt that I was now uniquely positioned to demonstrate this as the six sigma Champion had turned a manufacturing leader.

'How do we demonstrate that?' I thought.

As we were deliberating that, an opportunity presented itself. Mr Jeff Immelt was the president and CEO of GE Medical Systems worldwide, and he had a routine of visiting the entire manufacturing facilities worldwide once a year. His visit to the India facility was only a few months away.

'Why not redesign the entire manufacturing facility and process the six sigma way? Mr Immelt will see a dramatically different facility when he comes. This will encourage the corporate to move more products to be manufactured in India,' enthused DAP. He was a man in a hurry, always one step ahead of others.

'You can spend a million dollars to redesign the assembly line the six sigma way, if you need,' he assured us, 'but don't spend a nickel just because you want to.'

DAP kept his word and gave instructions to finance not to hold back on any expense we asked for. He just let us free to go and implement without breathing down our necks.

DAP was a classical example of an aggressive leader who knew how to extract the best performance from the team. He was so good in getting the famous GE 'stretch' goals achieved. His specialty was raising the goal bar as we were midway in execution. His logic was based on his fascination for pole vault. When a pole-vaulter is in mid-air and close to the bar, he is generating so much adrenaline. DAP felt that it could be leveraged by raising the bar a little more! DAP is an institution by himself and worth studying. I set out with my firebrand Black Belts, who toiled night and day to do something more. We felt that we could integrate the principles of design for six sigma with the Toyota Production System and create a world-class manufacturing facility. The

Toyota Production System, TPS, called for just-in-time inventory, lean manufacturing, and visual management system.

We tore down the old walls and the assembly line and replaced them with new ones. We analysed the inventory process and launched multiple six sigma projects; we built a forecast system tailor-made for our 'make-to-order' facility; we worked with the supplier base, including transportation and logistics.

When we finished, we had a beautifully laid-out assembly line, visible from any point, and all status information was displayed for anyone to see. More than the visual excellence, the six sigma projects resulted in profound improvement on the throughput of the facility, and we nearly doubled every parameter of interest!

We had a tradition of hoisting a green flag in the main hallway every Monday to celebrate on-time shipment. We had a fifty-two-week tracker table printed on a white board behind the flag, and we placed a green dot or red dot on it, depending on if we succeeded. We would get together as a team, hoist the flag, identify the hero of the week, and have pastries and coffee to celebrate. Due to all the six sigma efforts, we had maintained an unbroken record of 'on-time delivery' for all the preceding weeks. The tracker was full of green dots on the display.

Except the week when Mr Jeff Immelt visited us! It was red, as we had missed a shipment the previous week.

Jeff started his walkabout in the corridor surrounding the assembly lines. The walls had large glass windows to give a heightened visibility. As he was admiring all the great changes we had made to the assembly line, something else caught his eyes—a red flag flying. He looked at the red flag, the single red dot on the tracker, looked at the gleaming, super clean assembly lines, and smiled. 'So, you guys spent all the time and effort to prepare for my visit rather than making shipments?' he asked in half humour.

'It is all your fault, Mr Immelt,' I responded, and the entire gathering broke into peals of laughter. He was a big man who understood how his visits could affect the normal operations and moved on. But he just could not believe his own eyes as he stepped into the refurbished assembly line.

'What magic did you do, Paddy?' he asked. 'This was not like this last year.' DAP was quick to point out that we had redesigned the whole manufacturing system using six sigma principles. I stepped back and let my Master Black Belt explain the visual management system and all the improvement gains we had achieved. My functional manager was very displeased at this and gestured me to do the talking, but I ignored him.

'Paddy, how did you this?' Mr Immelt asked me again.

'I just let my team go and win, Jeff,' I answered sincerely. He understood it, nodded his head appreciatively, and moved on.

If there was one man outside the perimeter of the GEMS facilities who was keenly watching my progress, it was Mr Azim Premji, the recluse chairman of Wipro. He was a legend in India and continues to be one. The story of how he took over his father's two-million-dollar vegetable oil business and turned it into a multi-billon-dollar IT business was industry folklore. In spite of personal wealth worth multi-billion dollars, he lived a simple life. Stories of his taking a three-wheeler motorised rickshaw to work are a legend.

He was one of the richest men in India and perhaps with the most giving heart. He was the first wealthy Indian to sign the 'Giving Pledge', a campaign led by Bill Gates and Warren Buffet.

He had partnered with GE Medical Systems in setting up a manufacturing facility in Bangalore, and it was one of the three units under my jurisdiction. I enjoyed the rare honour of him reviewing our performance every quarter and was deeply impressed by his humility and laser focus on results. He did not brook any casualness among senior executives and was visibly upset when some meetings degenerated into events 'that kept the minutes but wasted the hours'. Everyone, including GE executives, took Mr Premji very seriously.

Mr Premji was keenly observing all the good we were doing under my leadership. CMM certification of the software unit, six sigma for IT, redesigned assembly lines integrating the six sigma and Toyota Production System all impressed him. He was always appreciative of me, and it was leading to a crescendo.

The main objective of redesigning the assembly line was to make it nimble, lean, and mean. DAP was not content with the appreciative nod from Jeff Immelt. In his typical fashion, he wanted to get a more business-oriented result. An opportunity presented itself.

One of our competitors had a lockout in their plant when their workers went on strike. DAP saw an opportunity to capture their market share by offering their clients GE products, exactly on the same day the competitor had committed. 'I want you to try and make as many CAT scanners as you can. I would love to see you double the output,' suggested DAP forcefully.

I protested mildly and half-heartedly, 'We are already halfway through the year, Prasanna. You know that our global suppliers need much longer lead time than that.'

It was typical DAP raising the bar midway; this meant that we had to manage the entire logistics and deliver one year's normal production in six months. Many felt that this was impossible without magic. I went to *all* the suppliers worldwide to persuade them to supply the parts with reduced lead time. Miracle did occur, and we delivered every piece demanded by DAP in an unheard of time span. Our new production line was really awesome.

These results earned our team the prestigious GE President's club award, and Mr Premji gave it away in a glittering ceremony. It was indeed the greatest honour of my life when I got to the stage to receive the award from Mr Premji. When he shook my hand appreciatively and remarked how he wished I were working for him at Wipro, I was floating on the proverbial cloud nine!

This refurbished plant became a big success and the topic of discussions in GE circles. We became the place to visit for American companies that wanted to set up a manufacturing base in India.

One of them was Delphi Automotive System's electronics division. This Indiana-based company wanted to set up an engineering software development centre in Bangalore. I conducted the visiting delegation around, explaining the dramatic changes we had accomplished. They were impressed and half-jokingly asked if I could join them to set up their Tech Centre India. 'You can get back to GE or wherever once it is done. We can arrange it as we are like a sister company to GE,' the visiting CEO said and smiled at me.

I took them on their offer, and they did manage to get GE agree to let me go; I joined them as their VP Operations and as their employee number three.

We started in a 'garage' mode, just the three of us in a small room, dreaming and planning to build a 500-people facility.

Clearly, the paradox principle 'if you want to win, let others win' worked very well for me; it sure would work for every one as well. What is more, this would be very relevant in personal lives too. We live our lives as family and as friends and buddies. We have a choice to thrust ourselves in front of every opportunity, assuming that we alone know how to be successful. Or, we have an option to let others work and win, which might be a better option.

In family life, as we age, we have an opportunity to step back and let our children shine in the limelight, instead of making everything about as and for us. Many of us make this terrible mistake to end up in agony, while all the joy and happiness is waiting to rush to us, if only we would step aside. This principle appears paradoxical not because it *is*, but because we don't do the right thing.

It was time for me to say one more goodbye; I was leaving GE world and joining Delphi Corp's Tech Centre. They were worlds apart from each other, truly representing their geographies. GE, with its Thomas

Alva Edison connection and Connecticut base was as aggressively innovative. Delphi, on the other hand, true to its pedigree as an ex-GM company and based out of Indiana, was carefully conservative.

It was time for this spinning gyroscope, me, to take a different bearing and navigate to new destiny. I got busy with the new job at Delphi, and as events moved me beyond, I discovered yet another paradox principle: *If you want to win, prepare to lose.*

IF YOU WANT TO WIN,
PREPARE TO LOSE.

CHAPTER 5

❧

You Will Drown in the Puddle

We all have a compelling need to win in whatever we attempt, and this drives us into a frenzy of action. This makes us very nervous, and we act as if we are possessed by some unknown demon. We are unable to think of anything else but getting the result we want, and this cuts into our peace of mind; we spend more time worrying about results than actually doing what is necessary to get them. This steals the precious time that would actually help in success.

We end up failing many times, accomplishing the very thing we very badly want to avoid. What can we do to avoid such a thing? What skills should we pick up to keep calm and stay focused on what we need to do without worrying about anything else?

This thought was seizing my mind as I started the first day in my new job. To be honest, I was not even looking to join any new company, let alone Delphi. By the time I was jokingly faulting Mr Immelt for missing my target in GE, I had completed nearly a decade in the manufacturing sector, away from the software industry.

The information technology industry was booming in India, propelled by the Y2K programs. The world had spent billions of dollars to correct the defect of the millennium. Everyone was worried that the 'date' variable in the programs will malfunction with the digits 'falling out of the program' due to a design flaw. Companies worldwide worked feverishly to get this corrected before the year 2000 was born. As millions of programs had to be corrected in a short time, clients hired Indian companies like TCS, Wipro, and Infosys to have the programs purged of that defect.

The scare felt by companies worldwide was so much that even the Mayan prediction of the end of the world paled in comparison. The Y2K modern man had no right to poke fun at the Mayans. The Mayans did not have a computer while the modern man did, and it was malfunctioning!

Even GE Medical Systems' products were not spared; we had to ensure that the embedded software running the ultrasound scanners functioned correctly at the dawn of the new millennium. OB/GYN doctors used them, and we could not risk the baby or its mother.

The New Year's Eve of year 2000 was the most memorable for me. It was not because of the grand parties that were going on all over; actually, *it was the year I did not celebrate at all*. As the head of the unit, I had to spend the entire night of 31 December 1999 keeping vigil during all the time zones of the world. We waited, clutching a satellite phone, just in case some doctor far away in the world tried to reach us. Luckily, our fix worked beautifully, and no one had any problem whatsoever. No one called. We just sacrificed the party of the millennium for the sake of bug of the millennium.

This experience spiked my interest in getting back to the IT sector. It was not only exciting but also came with bountiful salary. 'Why not start an IT services company myself?' asked my restless mind. I started doing what budding entrepreneurs do first—getting some potential clients to assure business.

When Delphi approached with a job offer, it appeared to be a perfect trial run for my ability to establish an IT services unit from the scratch. The expat CEO from United States had shown the carrot of my possible succession to the throne, and this was too tempting to refuse. Predictably, I delayed the plan of starting something of my own and joined them as their chief operating officer.

It was a rewarding experience, worth every ounce of the effort. We started small in a tiny office with just a couple of chairs, and went on to build a world-class facility of 30,000 square feet over nine months. All the while, we continued to hire engineers and train them.

Delphi had its functional tech centres in Singapore and Japan. Costs of these Far East centres were escalating, and this had prompted the idea of setting up the tech centre in India. But then, we had to compete with them to get the projects from the parent unit in the United States. This was complicating things for us, but we just had to deal with it.

We had to offer something that other centres could not do as a differentiator to win projects. We deliberated in our executive council meeting for long before I came out with a winning argument based on my GE experience. 'What we accomplished in the GE software centre, known as GSDC, was remarkable, which I would try to leverage,' I thought.

The GSDC unit in Bangalore was developing software that breathed life into GE's diagnostic imaging scanners like CAT, MRI, and CFD. It was a part of GEMS global technology operations and worked in tandem with similar units in Japan, France, and America.

'DAP' D. A. Prasanna, the president was a man of infinite optimism and matching energy. He had enormous patience and persistence to get the result he aimed for. Bringing this software development centre was his idea, and he was proud of it. He was known to think far ahead than anyone else.

In order to differentiate us from other GSDCs, DAP tasked us to get ourselves certified to CMM level 5 certification in one go. CMM level 5 was, and still is, the highest level of certification possible in the world. In the early the 1990s very few organisations had reached that level of quality in the world. It was as much a quintessential DAP as it was the famous GE stretch.

The CMM level certification programme has a very interesting history. The US Department of Defense had faced rampant delays and cancellation of projects wasting hundreds of millions dollars every year. DOD outsourced most of its work to private enterprise, and the software support industry was full of small shops— affectionately called mom and pop shops.

They were very concerned about this loss of moneys and programme delays. Sure enough, they launched a detailed investigation to find the cause and work out a mitigation plan. DOD discovered that engineers were treating software development as an art and not as an engineering process; they simply did not want to follow any strict regimen. In order to bring in the engineering rigour, DOD contracted with Carnegie Mellon University in Pittsburgh, Pennsylvania, to develop a process model that could reign in reluctant software engineers.

The university came out with the capability maturity model, CMM for short, through its SEI software engineering institute. DOD enforced this on its engineers and the vendors they contracted with.

But then, only those vendors working with DOD were getting themselves certified and that too just level 3, as it was the minimum criteria for doing business with DOD. A level 3 just meant that everyone was following the same work instructions. Level 5 meant that companies had to demonstrate a consistent behaviour of measuring and continuously improving themselves. This generally took several years—perhaps after a couple of failed attempts—that too aided by expensive specialist consultants.

At the time when DAP set the lofty goal of level 5 certification, GSDC did not even have a standardised process; every engineer followed his own process. SEI would sure have given them a 'level 0' certification, had they audited them! It was typical and audacious of DAP to set a goal *seemingly* out of touch with current ground reality. As can be expected no one liked that idea.

'Our maturity comes from GE's 100 years of innovation and excellence,' DAP declared. 'We are a company of standardisation and process. We have so many blue books that define each and everything we do. Above all, we are a six sigma company with unparalleled performance. Why should it be difficult for us to be recognised for *what we are doing already?*' he implored.

The trouble was, the GSDC geeks were reluctant participants in the six sigma projects. They, like every other programmer in the world, felt that software development was an *art*, which makes it individualistic and hence cannot be standardised. With such group thinking rampant, we now had CMM level 5 as the new goal. When I announced my plan for launching six sigma and CMM initiatives together, there was a revolt on my hands. Almost all of them declared that we did not know what we were talking about.

When I persisted on moving ahead, I was met with a chorus of 'We are bound to fail, and so why even try?' Many strongly felt that we should not be launching two initiatives together, as they were bound to confuse everyone.

'If we want to win, we should be prepared to lose,' I responded, without recognising that I was enunciating another paradox principle. That was catchy.

'But why take two at the same time? Why could we not do one at a time?' some wailed.

That was the opening I was looking for. That gave me an opportunity to prove that *one plus one is not two, not even one*. Some new math this. Changing people's minds always needed a game changer concept.

'Oh, by the way, these are not two separate initiatives but a single integrated initiative,' I countered.

I was met with a chorus 'How is that?'

It was time to explain how the six sigma fused in to the CMM model as a toolbox for measurement and continuous improvement. 'We all know that to get the highest level of certification, we need to establish a measurement system, use quantitative techniques to continuously improve quality.' Everyone agreed and there was no problem there.

'Don't you recognise this as *six sigma being spelt in English*?' I was beginning to make sense to them, and they listened with rapt attention as I pounded them with formidable logic. Slowly and steadily they started crossing over to my side, and vey soon I had the majority backing me up. 'So, do you all agree that they are not two initiatives but a single initiative?' I was almost teasing them.

'Well, we now see that it is a single programme, but why did you say that one plus one is not even one?' asked a young girl who remembered everything I had said.

'That is because, we are doing six sigma already in our company, and we have a very rigorous process orientation in whatever we do. What we need to do now is to just contextualise the two for the nature of work we do here. So, it is nothing new for us after all, making *one plus one being not even one*.' They all laughed with me at this fuzzy math. They always doubted my IQ, and this was confirming their view about me perhaps. They did not mind it and I did not care, and so we had an agreement.

It was a tough but intellectually rewarding exercise. The unit was full of very bright engineers, who loved intellectual contact sport. Once they were convinced, the young team swung into full gear and worked hard, preparing for a formal certification, which was only a year away. Being a GE entity, none of us believed that we needed any specialist consultant. DAP was indeed successful in hypnotising us.

The certification audit would simply look at two things. One, if the unit had documented the work instructions, if there were data analysis, and if the teams were able to predict and hence control future. Second, they would see if this was being consistently followed across the unit by all.

We were to be audited by a European audit agency with an impeccable record for integrity and rigour. We all expected the audit to be very tough and demanding. We did not take any chance and worked hard, drawing strength from the ubiquitous GE stretch. The audit day was fast approaching.

When the lead auditor heard about us, he was taken aback. How could we seek to be certified to the highest level at first go, without any consultant or any trial run? He just could not refuse to audit a *GE company*, and so he flew in from Mumbai with a five-day audit schedule; he was so sure that we would fail to withstand his scrutiny right at the start, he had booked his return on the night of the first day.

He made it a point to show me his return ticket when I received him at the airport.

'You may be a GE company, but it means nothing to me,' he told me sternly. 'No one has ever done what you are attempting. How can you even think of going in for level 5 certification in first go? I suggest you convert my audit into a pre-qualification audit so that you can avoid the embarrassment of failure.' He was visibly upset, though he meant well.

'I know GE does not take failures lightly and it may be good for your career too, to convert this into pre-qualification audit.' He went on to appeal to my good sense as he checked into the hotel. I looked directly into his eyes and told him that we surely will succeed and so he should not be concerned. 'How can you be so sure, considering no one has done it before?' he asked, a bit irritated.

'We are GE,' I replied. 'We always succeed because we are always prepared to fail.' He dismissed it as empty rhetoric and pressed me again to change the audit. I refused.

'Your wish,' he said curtly; he wished me good night and went to bed.

As I drove back home, the entire struggle, debates, and hard work flashed through my mind. GE has such a demanding environment that there is a time multiplier effect. Things generally happen faster at GE than anywhere else.

One has to work in a GE company to understand this. There have been so many firsts in the company, which have been firsts in the industry. GE had so many 'achievement accelerators' like the GE stretch, lack of boundaries, and speed as a value, which help one achieve extraordinary results in a short time.

The audit started on a sombre note with the lead auditor explaining the procedure to the team leads and the customary caution that I should stay out of the process. 'If you even clear your throat when I am seeking answers from others, you will be disqualified,' he warned.

He shared his plan to return to Mumbai that night itself with the team. 'It is very unexpected that anyone will be ready to be straight away qualified to level 5, and so don't feel disappointed if I find you not ready today. I have my return ticket booked, and here it is for you to see.'

No wonder that the team felt very discouraged, but I ignored all the angry glances they threw at me.

He started his methodical audit without much ado, and it was a gruelling day. Much to his pleasant surprise, the lead auditor liked what he saw during the audit and decided to extend the return flight by a day. He liked what he saw on the second day, and that made him change the ticket again. He kept postponing the return by a day every day, till he completed all the five days of audit he had originally planned. He was very surprised by his own decision.

The audit was finally over, and the team was clearly exhausted. With mixed feelings of anxiety and expectations, the team trooped into the conference hall to hear his customary concluding remarks.

He started explaining his sense of irritation that he felt on the first day at being asked to perform assessment audit on a company that was not ready as far as he was concerned. The pulse of the team leads rose, and everyone could hear others' hearts pounding. What would be his final comments?

He kept us lingering on the thought of possible failure and continued to narrate how many companies had overestimated themselves, only to fail in the audit. He talked a great deal about his long experience and sage counsel that haste always made waste.

'Where do you folks stand in all this?' He appeared to be grave when he said that. Our hearts almost stopped. Then he suddenly broke in smiles.

'I have no hesitation in recommending that you qualify for a level 5 certification,' he declared to a loud applause. 'This by itself is extraordinary, as I usually play it by the chest and don't share my findings directly. But what I saw here was truly extraordinary.'

DAP stood vindicated. Again. This reverberated in the United States, even in the software engineering institute of Carnegie Mellon University. My Master Black Belt who had spearheaded the audit was invited to talk and share our experience there.

That extraordinary experience raced through my mind as I was looking at putting India tech centre at the centre of the Delphi global map.

'How could I leverage that GE experience at Delphi Tech Centre?' I thought as we continued our debate in the management council.

'Yes, this must be it. We will author a quality system work instructions that combined the provisions of capability maturity model and six sigma. Our products control air bags, brakes, and engines in cars. So we will address passenger safety considerations also. No other tech centres in Delphi world has done this. We will be delivering the highest quality and reliability at unbelievable price points. This will be our differentiator,' I said as I addressed the bright engineers.

My CEO was very pleased as he had not planned to be that aggressive. This was going to be not only a differentiator, but it would also give us an opportunity to teach the parent unit in Indiana. They were not so focused on software process as much as they were on the engineering process. And no six sigmas. A typical American mom and pop shop problem there.

It would be like tail wagging the dog!

So with gusto we went to work to create the quality system and train our engineers first on the software process and then on the standard Delphi engineering process, using some internal dummy projects. This went on for a couple of months, and soon it was time to take on the world, the Delphi world.

We took a batch of engineers to our global headquarters at Kokomo, Indiana, purportedly for getting them trained in the products that were being designed. This was innocuous enough and was something our headquarters was insisting anyway. They had to teach the 'colonies', hadn't they?

My CEO and I, on the other hand, had a hidden agenda. We wanted to teach the masters our software process. It was both funny and ironical that we both wanted to teach something to the other.

Before we left India, my manager was in a dilemma. On the one hand, he was happy that I was putting his India tech centre on the map. On the other hand, he was not sure if I would actually deliver. What if I was full of bravado without substance and it fell flat on the experienced technical managers in our HQ at Kokomo?

I was very clear in my mind about two things. One, I was sure of what I was talking about, and two, I knew from my experience that *if we want to win, we must prepare to lose.*

And sure I was prepared to lose. This had taken the entire *pressure of having to succeed* off my chest, and I could focus on preparing to do what we had planned to do. But how was I to carry along the engineers in India and Indiana? IT developers always felt that each one of them had a unique gift that cannot be the result of a work instruction or a *process*. I had to approach the process paradigm differently.

'What do you do when you come to work?' I asked them rhetorically, and I wrote down how work actually flows on a day-to-day basis. 'It is what we call as *workflow*. The programs you write will have to meet boundary conditions under which to operate; they will have to meet some safety and security conditions, and finally achieve some specific results. You will also measure certain things to see how well the program codes behave. Finally you would discuss some management aspects of the project with multiple departments associated with the work. Are you with me?' I checked to see if they were still listening to me.

This made perfect sense to them, and they were willing to hear more and participate. I then went on to create a 'clickable' flow chart with links in every box and connected them with process documents. By doing so, I shifted the emphasis to the way they worked with process documents as *aide-memoir*, rather than process documents dictating what they should do. This shifted the whole game of process becoming an *aid* rather than a hated rule book. This 'clickable flow chart' was what I was to present to the senior executives at HQ. The president and the chief technology officer were very impressed to see what we had accomplished in such a short time. For them, the foray into India was to tap into the low-cost technical talent support, and now they were getting much higher-value advice in return.

I then took the upper hand in the conversation. 'This way, you can ensure discipline, consistency, and six sigma rigour in product development. This should be your blue book, and we from India tech centre will be happy to help you implement this here.' My CEO beamed as I concluded. 'Mind you, we have put the engineering workflow at the centre, instead of bureaucratic rules.' I reminded.

The president was curious about something about me. He was wondering how a new employee, however experienced, could dare to come to the global headquarters to teach a thing or two.

'How on earth did you pick up the courage, coming from a start-up subsidiary, to teach us?' he asked half jokingly and half seriously. 'What if you had failed to convince us?'

'Plain and simple,' I answered. 'I was mentally prepared to fail, and so it did not scare me. Where the scare leaves, courage enters.' The president laughed aloud. He sure was good in seeing value when he saw some. He started popularizing us among various divisions of the company across United States, stressing that we had the best quality system in the world. 'Better than even Japan,' he would always say.

We continued our sales pitch, offering India tech centre, visiting many divisions across America. It was a gruelling cross-country ride across much of the US Midwest. Powered by the lower costs and hard-working labour force, Midwest states had emerged as the manufacturing belt in America. Driving through the sparsely populated towns and miles of farmlands was an experience by itself, as we hurtled down the freeway.

It was a bit scary to be driving around in the tornado alley in that season. It was not named 'tornado alley' for nothing; there had been several tornado touchdowns in that area. The funnel clouds barrelling down with ferocity, spinning like a giant top, and throwing large eighteen-wheeler trucks far as if they were toys were only good to see in movies. You don't want to be anywhere near them.

With all the drama over, we returned to India vastly satisfied. Thanks to all the hard selling we had done, project contracts started flowing from the United States, and we got terribly busy. We hired more, trained more, and executed more. Things were getting better and better, and the euphoria of success was building up in my mind.

We, in general, seem to have selective vision; we see only what we want to see. What is more important, we see only what we seek; this psychological limitation leads to what is colloquially called a blinkered vision. For example, we rarely notice that extreme emotions invariably come as twins. A big win always has a tinge of sorrow—maybe a bad feeling that other dear ones did not succeed or get it. An extremely joyous moment is accompanied by a bit of miserable feeling about something associated with it.

Like darkness in a flame.

It was not surprising to me at all that I started feeling a bit lost among all the success we were building in the tech centre. *Tail wagging the dog* feels good until the tail starts feeling that *it should be the dog*, really speaking. If Kokomo had to learn from Bangalore, why was the role reversed? 'Why should I be a subservient guru?' I mused.

Even before I joined the tech centre, the urge to take control of my destiny was working on me a lot. Jack Welch had constantly urged all of us, the employees of GE worldwide, to control our destinies. 'Control your destiny or someone else will' was his common refrain.

The Y2K program that we had managed in GE started haunting my memory again. What a problem it was that shook the entire world!

The engineers who had designed the computer programs in the early part of the twentieth century represented a year in two digits, i.e. as 98, 99, instead of 1998, 1999. This meant that computer programs would move to year 00 instead of 2000 at the end of 1999. The users would be in no position to differentiate between 1900 and 2000. The program's calculations might see a 00, and could interpret it as 1900 or 2000.

The whole world spent billions of dollars to check all the programs that ran in any computing device and alter the program to change all year representations to four digit numbers. This would ensure that 1900 and 2000 could be clearly distinguished.

Our engineers had done such a great fix, it worked worldwide without a single hitch. That was the greatness of a GE company. Zero defect, six sigma. Jack Welch won that day.

Those two years had made such a big impact on me that I was seriously considering starting an IT company of my own. Some of my friends felt that it was foolish to make that leap of faith, particularly after spending nearly a decade in manufacturing industry. They were sure that it was doomed to fail.

But then, my life strategy was founded on paradox principles, and for those who scared me, my response was to throw one at them. 'If you want to succeed, prepare to lose,' I retorted. I kept going and started working on founding a company and started establishing contacts with potential clients in the United States and some upcoming IT companies in India.

There were a couple of IT companies that were making waves in Bangalore, Wipro Technologies and Infosys Technologies. Of the two, Infosys was the cynosure of all eyes in India. 'Why not write to them and seek opportunities to deliver services?' I thought. 'But whom do I start with?' I rummaged my table drawers and found the business card of one Mr Shibulal of Infosys. I sat and closed my eyes to recall how I had met Shibulal a few months back.

The iconic 'NRN' Narayana Murthy, who shook the corporate firmament in India, founded Infosys. His vision of creating a globally respected corporation which would create wealth ethically and share it with all stakeholders was the biggest story in India for very long. And he walked the talk, with outstanding value delivered to clients, creating ESOP millionaires among employees and driving enormous charitable work.

This successful billionaire had a strange start in free market capitalism. He started as a European socialist, was soon disillusioned, and returned to India from France. Unlike some socialists who end up as vulture capitalists, he redefined socialism as 'creating wealth and sharing with stakeholders,' rather than redistributing the available wealth. He was, in a way, answering Churchill's criticism that capitalism was unequal sharing of wealth, while socialism was equal sharing of poverty!

At the break of the new millennium, Infosys was only a few thousand people strong with a revenue of a couple of hundred million dollars. But it had made hundreds of employees ESOP millionaires.

More than all these success stories, NRN's articulation of value system in simple, actionable terms was extraordinary. 'Clearest conscience is the softest pillow,' he would say, or 'If in doubt, disclose.' It made everyone understand values directly and follow.

While he created so much of wealth, he would always urge, 'Power of money is the power to give.' He meant it, and Infosys established a charitable foundation to help the needy and the poor. This was contagious, and many of the senior managers of Infosys followed suit and were doing their own personal charity.

The legend of Infosys founding is so romantic that it became a modern-day Robin Hood story. He and six of his friends left well-paying jobs and pawned their wives' jewellery to raise 250 dollars as seed capital. They just went on to grow the company into a multi-billion-dollar enterprise with a market capitalisation of over *thirty billion dollars. All in about twenty years!*

Naturally, Infosys became a 'must-visit' facility for the organisations in Bangalore. So we went from the Delphi Tech Centre to see for ourselves how this *small 200-million-dollar company* was shaking up the world. The visit was managed by the smooth-talking Infosys team leader, who said all the right things, cracked the right self-deprecating jokes, and with a tinge of false humility, spoke gloriously about the company. We were ushered into a spacious conference room to meet one of the co-founders of Infosys, Mr Shibulal. There was much banter and humour as we waited for him to arrive.

Soon enough, he walked in, immaculately dressed, welcomed us in his accented voice, and talked about how they had started the company. After the pleasant conversation, we exchanged our business cards and left. This was the card that was staring back at me as I looked at it. 'Should I reach out to him?' I thought hard and decided to connect with him anyway.

So I wrote to him, seeking partnership for a company that I was yet to start, like I wrote to many others in the United States and India. Many of the potential US clients responded favourably. The clients were all exhausted after spending half a trillion dollars to fix the Y2K bug. Taking undue advantage, many vendors had fleeced them as the dead line—31 December 1999—approached. They were in urgent need to find some small vendor who was willing to play at the lowest price.

They could not get anyone smaller than me. I did not even have a company at that time! No wonder I had an overwhelming response from the then prospective clients.

While everyone else responded in a predictable manner, Mr Shibulal reached back with a counter proposal. He argued that it was a wrong time to start any company as the dot-com bubble had just then burst. He was on the lookout for professionals with an entrepreneurial mindset. 'You should be joining me at Infosys,' he urged.

It was a puzzling response, and I decided to validate his premise. It was the year 2001. NASDAQ was hovering around 1,500 after blazing to a peak of 5,100 on 10 March 2000. The NASDAQ climbed to a dizzy 5,100 from a mere 1,000 in 1997, fuelled by the dot-com boom, when literally hundreds of start-up companies were launched without any well-defined revenue model. The *World Wide Web* craze had hit the world completely.

The World Wide Web was invented in 1990, and by 1993 it started catching the imagination of companies. It can be understood as an electronic bulletin board, on which any company could display its products and services. It made things easier for ordinary mom and pops to view and buy them. The companies that advertised their goods and services made money as customers bought them. But what about the companies that had set up the computers that hosted the websites? Since it was intended for the 'common man', access to websites was free. No one paid for using the World Wide Web. How would the dot-com companies that set up the websites make money?

A vast majority of dot-com companies did not have any other avenue to make money. The common notion was that websites would attract so many visitors and advertisement revenue would pour in a deluge. In short, they thought they owned some electronic version of billboards of the Super Bowl or IPL finals!

This 'build, they will come' concept failed miserably, and most of the dot-com companies burnt out the initial funding they had gotten from venture capitalists and were living on borrowed money.

To drive the last nail on their coffin, the US federal bank raised interest rates six times during the period from 1999 to early 2000, making borrowed moneys very expensive. The dot-com bubble simply burst, and hundreds of companies went bankrupt while thousands were acquired by regular or conventional companies, whom the dot-coms had derisively called as 'brick and mortar' companies.

This dot-com burst happened just soon after the Y2K boom, and as a consequence, very many IT services companies were scaling down and shuttering. No one needed that many code writers any more. The IT services market was staring at a glut. Considering all this, Mr Shibulal's counter offer made a lot of sense, and so I reluctantly agreed to meet him for a job interview.

It was not clear what position I was being considered for, as I wasn't applying for any in the first place. I had sent in my resume stressing my accomplishment in GE as six sigma Champion, with particular emphasis on six sigma for IT. My expectation was that as an IT services organisation, Infosys would welcome me.

The resume was circulated internally and was promptly rejected. *It was not their fault at all.* I did not have any formal quality function experience, and everyone knew that quality champions from the GE world were more business guys. To cap it all, I was coming with a long diverse experience covering multiple functions, none of which was quality.

I was nevertheless upset and called Shibulal to berate him that Indian companies had a limited view of things and that was why I was reluctant to apply in the first place. He pacified me and insisted I come down to meet him and another co-founder. They would give a patient hearing, he assured me. He was somehow keen on bringing me on board.

And so I went, now more determined than ever to reject the potential job offer, telling myself that I was only going to honour a founding member of Infosys. 'It just won't work,' I kept telling myself. I was greeted by the VP HR at the reception and was escorted to meet Shibulal and his board colleague Mr Dinesh.

They were very pleasant and respectful and started the strange interview for a job that was non-existent, that too for a person who was not keen. Both the founders were respectful and humble even under my extreme provocation; it was a part of their value system.

I would see this time and time again over several years with them. The founders had learnt how to keep their heads on their shoulders; they were unpretentious and simple, not withstanding what they had collectively achieved. Their success in making Infosys bellwether gave birth to the middle-class entrepreneurship in India.

I would witness this play out many times later. Like when Dinesh sent his limo at Mangalore airport to drop an old man who was sitting next to him in the flight and took a shared taxi with us to ride to office. Or see Shibu help so many without revealing his identity. Humility and being respectful were ingrained in their character, and it seeped into Infosys value system.

On the other hand, being over-assertive was my nature, and it was no wonder that our conversations went out of sync in the interview room right at the start. I started by explaining what Infosys ought to be doing to become a true global corporation. It must have sounded very bizarre for the HR leader to see the iconic founders getting 'lectured' in that manner. If it was, he did not show it either. For their part, Shibu and Dinesh continued to be polite and respectful.

It sure did strike strange to me that they did not try to cut me short. They listened patiently without interrupting me. Slowly, our conversation drifted towards the fundamental way of transforming organisations, and Shibulal asked me to list three hurdles Infosys faced in my view. I had thought deeply about this before I came in for the interview and was ready. He had already shared the Infosys vision of building a globally respected corporation while he was enticing me to join him.

'There are three things you need to do, and you will struggle in all the three,' I started. 'First, you must inculcate the concept of a corporation. Second, you need to balance loyalty with high performance, and finally your software process must address process variations.'

'Why do you think we lack them or we will have difficulty?' asked Shibu, as if to prime me to talk forthrightly.

'Your employees are not likely to understand what a corporation is. Your business model is based on smaller teams getting assembled for short-duration projects at multiple client locations in the world,' I said, taking the cue. 'They form, execute, dissolve, and join some other project team. Their horizon is limited to tactical needs of the project they are working on, and as they grow in the organisation, they do not scale their thinking beyond projects. This repeats itself forever, as long as they are in the organisation. So, they never understand what a corporation is.

'Two, you have been spectacularly successful in building teams with young engineers fresh from school. This helps you to keep the operational cost low. Over a period of time, these youngsters learn, enhance their knowledge, and grow up to occupy senior positions. This model gets so venerated as they achieve higher margins due to lower operational costs. But you pay a price here. Anyone joining from another organisation will struggle to get integrated and respected. This means your ability to acquire experiential wisdom from outside is restricted.'

Shibu and Dinesh kept listening, although it was obvious to me that Dinesh wanted to move the conversation from management speak about quality. He was a project and process management guy, and my pontificating perhaps made no sense at all.

'Finally, all your software development process measurement is based on averages and not standard deviation. This means any improvement that you claim cannot be statistically proven to be significant.' I smiled as I finished my case and paused.

'How do you say that we cannot prove our improvement to be statistically significant?' It was Dinesh asking now. This was obviously his pet theme, and he was curious to know what made me say that.

'You need to integrate six sigma with your process model,' I replied. 'Measure the standard deviation of the variables of interest, besides mean. Any decision you make based on averages is open for questioning. In achieving clarity, standard deviation rules, and that is why you need to implement six sigma,' I said forcefully.

Dinesh was a bit surprised at that. 'After visiting many world-class companies that were doing six sigma, we have concluded that six sigma stat tools are not applicable to IT services industry. Why bother about process variability and standard deviation when these techniques are not applicable?' he asked emphatically.

This was not new to me, having faced it before in GE and Delphi. 'I can prove you wrong right now and here,' I suggested and looked at him inquisitively. He did not say anything, and I took it for a yes. 'Suppose a six-footer was walking towards his village and came across a large puddle of water. A guy sitting near that pond says that the depth was about four feet average. Can the six footer walk across the pond?' I asked rather belligerently.

'Of course he could,' retorted Dinesh. 'You said he was six foot plus,' he added, closing it proudly.

'*He would drown, Mr Dinesh,*' I said. 'Average may be four feet, but the depth has variations across the pond, and the depth could be even twelve feet at some point and he would drown in the pond.'

There was total silence for a few minutes. Dinesh got up, shook hands with me and parted. 'We will have to think carefully about your suitability at Infosys. You have an impressive background and have worked with great leaders, but we will have to see how we can use that.' He gave his trademark flashy grin and left.

After an awkward silence, I picked up my laptop bag and bid goodbye to Shibu. 'I suspect you suffer from what we call as NIH syndrome "not invented here". You feel that anything not invented by you is not good enough. This prevents companies from becoming great,' I ranted. I was sure they would not make a job offer.

Shibu let me vent my feelings and said, 'I concede we don't know all this, and we need people like you to join us if we are to become global. Why don't you join us?' he asked. I was taken aback at that. After the explosive interview, for a job role that was not clear, and even after my rants, he was asking me to join him.

'It won't work, Shibu,' I said. 'I don't think Infosys is ready to induct people like me.'

'Walk with me to my office,' he said. 'It is a couple of hundred feet away in another building. Let us have a talk there.' He put his arms around me and walked me to his office.

The interview and the few hundred steps we took made a big impression on me. Here were two gentlemen who were iconic founders of Infosys—so respectful and humble even when the interaction was not going the right way.

Shibu's gesture of walking me to his office with his arm around my shoulder was also very touching. As we settled in his office, he talked of their vision and the challenges they faced and the struggle to get there.

'You need a healthy infusion of folks from global corporations. Many of us who have had the opportunity to transform organisations bring in the expertise,' I emphasised what I had said earlier in one breath.

'Which is the biggest first hurdle you face in any organisational transformation?' he asked with an innocent face.

'Resistance to change, of course!' I said. 'We face it all the time, and we know how to deal with it, while you may not.'

'In which case, why are you put off if we don't accept your hypothesis or the solutions for us? Either you join us, break our resistance, and transform us, or accept that you were merely posturing as a change leader. We can wish each other well and go our respective ways. You cannot claim to be a change leader and yet get upset if we resist the change you want to bring in.' He had trapped me well with that argument, and there was no escape.

I had to accept this as very valid and consented to consider a job offer. With all pleasantries, we bid goodbye and went our ways. I waited for the job offer to show up.

Apparently, the tribulations were not over just yet. When the job offer landed in my hands, I was shocked to find that it reduced my compensation—some 40 per cent less than what I was getting. I thought it was some typo and rushed back to the HR head, but he assured me that it was indeed a right offer.

To compound that, the role did not have any job description either, and I was not sure what this offer was for. When I confronted Shibu with this, he declared grandly that leadership roles did not come with any job description, only managerial roles did. 'As a leader you find out whatever needs to be done and just do it!'

This was the most winning argument I ever heard, and I fell for it and started wondering if I should accept a job offer that reduced my pay by 40 per cent!

It was my wife who played a very crucial role in that decision. She impressed a reluctant me that life was not lived with just money; when I created an excel sheet to show how our net worth could erode over five years, she remarked, 'You sure know how to run a simulation model, but I know how to run the family with any income. Trust me with it and accept the job offer.'

That was that, and I joined Infosys.

Little did I foresee that the next ten years would be a roller coaster that would launch me into the concluding lap of the Bangalore-Boston marathon, provide stock options that would bring in financial rewards never even dreamt, and would launch our entire family on to the immigration path to become US citizens. The kids would grow up as independent American kids, our daughter marrying a very bright young man, son conquering the math league of New England, and my wife capturing the minds of the Norfolk county schools.

We let go what we cherished—our comfortable salary, position, a hometown known for forty years— and went West to Boston. We sailed in the new '*Mayflower*', a Lufthansa flight, like the old Pilgrims from England did. We landed at Boston Logan, not very far from the Wampanoag village of Providence where the Pilgrims had landed.

We went through the tough times like them and were helped by the locals, just as the Pilgrims were. We worked hard with indomitable will to succeed and make America our new homeland.

We were mentally prepared to lose. And so we succeeded.

IF YOU WANT TO BE THERE,
BE HERE.

CHAPTER 6

—⁓—

Thirty Yards Make Nine Thousand Miles

Never did I anticipate that those thirty yards that I walked with Shibu to his office would eventually take me 9,000 miles away to Boston, but it happened. Not only did those thirty yards take me that far, they led to a sequence of events that made me travel across the North American continent like the old gold prospectors. It was more than 'Westward, Ho!' for me.

The number of frequent-flyer miles that I accumulated financed several intercontinental holidays. The number of free nights I had collected meant that I had free rooms for all my holidays with family for several years. The travel around United States and Canada was so intense, that many days I would wake up confused, not knowing where the bathroom door was; I would walk half asleep and knock myself into a wall. Well, the door was 'there' the other day, in another city, in another hotel!

I was straddling the United States and Canada, constantly engaged in seeking new business opportunities, building high-performance teams, and trying to achieve something considered too difficult, if not impossible.

How does one retain sanity and self-confidence when faced with tough demands one after another? What are the skills, capability or tools should one acquire? I found the answer in the *most read dialogue* in human history.

No, it was not Plato's dialogue, but another dialogue written by another writer whose existence was never proved, but who was venerated as God's avatar nevertheless. It is a dialogue between a cowherd who was convinced he was God, and his supposedly brave prince cousin, who was trembling like a dry leaf in a battlefield.

It is part of the Mahabharata epic, called Bhagwat Gita or God's discourse.

The setting is surreal with Krishna, the lovable cowherd, discoursing in the midst of a battlefield. Yes, that was what he was doing, egging his buddy Arjuna, a reluctant warrior, to fight for *dharma* or righteous cause. In his view, not taking sides in a righteous war was as bad as taking the side of *adharma* or non-righteous cause. As it happens often, people very close to us do take wrong sides, even knowingly for a reason of their own, and those fighting for the right cause face a dilemma in fighting them. Arjuna had to fight his relatives and his own guru who had taught him warfare.

The crux of Krishna's arguments appeared to be centred on just one single point—*just live in the moment, and for the moment.* He harangues over eighteen chapters, elaborating this point in several different ways in a rather boastful way. He kind of makes it a sine qua non for success, some sort of psychological preparation to minimise anxiety neurosis.

Simply but paradoxically told—*if you want to be there, be here*. This was the way I understood that and used it as the guiding principle, as a decade of unpredictable, abruptly changing career moves hit me.

The starting point for all these happened in Bangalore and it was all about *a Saturday brunch*. To be more precise, a request to end the Saturday brunches made by the then CEO of Infosys, Nandan Nilekani.

'Can you stop this Saturday brunch for me, please?' he asked as I introduced myself upon joining Infosys.

After the star power of the prime founder Narayana Murthy, Nandan was the man with charisma. Tall, well-provided, he projected his personality very well. He had the proverbial gift of the gab and could charm anyone. And yes, he had the trademark humility, simplicity, and approachability that is common among all Infosys founders.

The founders had their own job division philosophy. 'NRN' Narayana Murthy was the ringmaster, orchestrating the entire show, when he was not too busy advising the kings and queens of the world. Infosys was his dream child, his middle child, 'in between his daughter and son' according to him. He shook the conscience of the Indian corporate world in early 1980s when he declared his vision of *creating a globally respected corporation that would create wealth ethically and share with all stakeholders*. Not many respected Indian companies at that time; nor did any company share ethically created wealth with anyone in those days.

It required Machiavellian or Chanakyan audacity of Murthy to think that way, and it made him the darling of the Indian middle class. This disillusioned socialist has created more millionaires than Carnegie ever did.

Nandan was the CEO, focusing on the sales function. With his charisma and silver tongue, he charmed the clients and prospects. He had his own vision that was larger than Infosys; he had a vision for his country and often talked about leveraging technology to root out some persistent problems that the poor of India faced.

Kris was the Geek of the team playing the technology guru; his fascination and artful ability in mastering any new technology or gadget was legendary. He took the responsibility of founding and growing Infosys Labs, a prime engine for innovation.

Shibu was the Jack Welch of the team. With his ferocious focus on execution excellence, he delivered on the discipline. Keeping Infosys relevant to the changing needs of the market was his passion.

Dinesh was the puritan of the team, and no wonder he was responsible for quality, process, and project management.

In his zeal for promoting quality, Dinesh constantly applied pressure on the team by maintaining that they were not delivering acceptable quality and failing in continuous improvement goals. NRN would have none of it and called for Saturday brunch meetings for hot seat reviews. Who would love to hear an earful on weekends instead of spending time with loving family?

'Shibu says he has brought in a tiger from the GE world, and I hope you don't let him down,' Nandan told me when I met him the first time after my joining. 'He tells me that your first assignment is to internalise the quality system in delivery organisation. If you do your job well, I expect Murthy's Saturday brunch meetings to stop. So my measure for your success is the number of brunches I am able to skip,' said Nandan with a twinkle in his eyes. He was very good in taking complex issues and presenting them in a simple way for everyone to comprehend.

No complex equations, no fancy pitch this—just the number of Saturday brunches per month as the measure of quality performance! That was classic Nandan. It was easy to understand, and no special tools were needed. Just count the number of brunches! I promised it would be done and got back to Shibu to brief him on this strange performance measure.

Nandan was the walking proof of the sales adage that 'if you cannot say in a few words, you probably don't have anything significant to say at all'.

Over the next three weeks, Shibu took me through several group meetings to give me a sense of what was going on in the organisation. What struck me during all the meetings was the laser focus on process. Every manager was measuring and reporting every aspect of *how* things were done. This gigantic exercise on the 'how' of things was being shepherded by the corporate quality managers who worked so hard and diligently to ensure process compliance.

Then the meeting with the great man NRN himself happened. It was the monthly review meeting. He was on full force and was highly critical of delivery, based on the performance reports from quality. It was clear that the sales and delivery teams were on the defensive, unable to counter the big man's torrential critique.

As I sat there watching, it was amazing to see what I had mentioned in the interview play out. The reports were all based on measuring and comparing averages and without any statistical proof for degradation of performance. And yet there we were, the big man hitting hard at the leadership, demanding improvements.

'Improve what?' I kept thinking. I just could not hold myself back, but Shibu restrained me, signalling that I should listen and observe in the first meeting.

After the explosive meeting was over, we walked back to his office silently, and I just could not wait to pounce on him for restraining me. 'Why did you not let me counter him?' I asked indignantly. 'You hired me for this very reason, and yet you did not let me do my job. There were many things that NRN said that could have been disputed,' I poured out in anger.

'Shooting from the hip does not help, baba,' he responded, using his favourite expression. 'You need to settle down first, understand what is going on in different areas of the company before you are ready to tackle the chairman of the board. You don't even know what is growing under your own feet yet, and yet you are impatient to get there. If you create a wrong impression in first encounter, it tends to stick forever. First impression is really the best impression you can create at this level of leadership. In fact that is the *only impression* you will be able to create. So better be *here* to learn what is going on before you pounce on him there in the boardroom,' he counselled.

The last statement struck me like a thunderbolt. I could paraphrase that conversation and use it as one more paradox principle to guide me: *'If you want to be there, be here!'* It was almost as if the Cheshire cat had come to life out from Alice in Wonderland's story and spoken to me. After all, the Cheshire cat had indeed advised Alice that the path to choose depended on where she wanted to go. No wonder, if you wanted to go there, you had to be *here at the right fork.*

The 'there' of what we were contending with was pretty clear to me. It had to be 'redefining the IT services performance paradigm' and 'transfer the ownership to the operational units from the corporate'. I would clearly know that we have reached 'there', once those brunch meetings that Nandan hated so much stopped.

But what was the 'here' in that context? As a newcomer, I sure did not fully know what was going on and needed to find out. Shibu was right.

As advised by him, I started focusing on understanding the lay of the land and gain an understanding of why we got into that situation to start with. Why did the delivery organisation get defensive and was almost unable to either meet the expectation or push back? Was it because they were doing a poor job or was it more because they did not know how to measure themselves and report appropriately?

Why would an organisation that had achieved the highest level of global quality certification even have a conversation around terrible quality issues? The way NRN was talking, it appeared as if customers were all getting very upset over the deliveries and were ready to jump ship and go to the competition. That was not the case at all; on the contrary, customers were so happy that almost all them kept coming back to get served by Infosys.

It was very puzzling to me, almost to the point of seeming bizarre, to see the corporate quality function holding total ownership of the quality processes and steering the delivery units. I began to wonder how one could be accountable without any ownership.

How can legislators and law enforcement hold only citizens accountable for a mile of cars pile-up on the interstate, even though the citizens had followed the traffic rules set by them? Everyone was completely dedicated and sincere, and yet somehow things were going awry according to the reports. It was a priceless learning that good intentions by themselves do not guarantee good results.

But the more interesting aspect that came out of a detailed analysis was that they *were not delivering poor quality at all.* And yet there was concern and anxiety eating the senior executive team. What was going on?

'We are humble and paranoid,' explained Shibu as I raised this aspect with him. 'Actually, we are humble because we are paranoid,' he added. 'We clearly recognise that we are growing too rapidly, have a globally dispersed team, and the market needs keep changing always. Many things can go wrong, and in fact, many things do go wrong.'

I mentally validated what he was explaining as he continued to talk. It was indeed true that as a global IT outsourcer, Infosys had its thousands of employees scattered all over the world, assisting clients in smaller teams. And the technology was changing rapidly in the marketplace. But I wondered why he did not mention that Infosys was hiring from engineering schools in thousands, perpetually dragging the average experience down. Was he in denial about this?

I thought too soon.

'On the top of all this, we hire thousands of young bright engineers from the best colleges and inject them into the teams, persistently reducing the experience profile of the teams. How do you ensure that our deliveries to clients are of world-class quality? Clients leave IBM and Accenture to work with us because of the best quality we deliver. If that is affected, we lose the business itself,' he concluded.

It was my turn to talk. 'In GE, they taught us that behavioural changes of very large teams are wrought by environmental control. Mere instructions will not help. Infosys teams are dispersed and are project oriented but not organisation oriented. Projects and team composition keep changing. So the environmental factors have to be ingrained in the team members' minds. This cannot be achieved by any rule book.'

'Of course, we recognise that,' he interjected quickly. 'The question to you is how do we do that?' Shibu was very clear why he had hired me. Pontification was clearly out. Getting into the ditch and getting hands dirty was in.

'Falling back on GE learning again, we must build an ecosystem that delivers a *violent feedback* for any transgression. And we must *transfer* the ownership to operations team from any corporate function. That is the key,' I concluded.

'People resist change,' he reminded me. 'The more successful a company is, the more resistant they become to change. We are a global icon today and financially very successful. No one will listen to you,' he prophesied.

'We jolt the organisation with paradigm shifts, catch them by surprise, and it will break the thick layer of resistance. It will take a while for them to even understand that. People listen *when we offer what they don't have, and which they seek very badly.*'

I stopped and looked at him. Shibu looked pleased; it appeared that he was feeling more comfortable about bringing me on board. 'Wear me as your bulletproof vest in your gunfights,' he said as a parting advice. 'You will need it.'

He paused and added, 'Often.'

I set out to think of a game plan to drive ownership change as well as paradigm shift. Shibu had already created a Delivery Excellence structure within the delivery organisation with a manager nominee from every service line. They acted as sort of liaison between service lines and corporate quality that was laser-focused on establishing the 'how' of things.

'Follow the judo method,' my inner voice commanded. The fundamental idea behind judo was not to fight the opponent's strength directly as you would surely lose, but rather let the opponent deploy his strength but you deflect that and make him lose balance and fall. In other words, the tactic was deflection rather than resistance.

The legendary Kano San devised it as something larger than a martial art. It was a type of self and social development, as it was truly a combination of Confucius philosophy and *Jita Kyoei*—principle of mutual benefit.

So if the organisation had used the quality champions structure in delivery to deploy its inspection regime, I would not dismantle it but deflect it. I decided to use the very same structure to change the entire paradigm in both form and content.

I must thank the judo master Kano San for helping me understand this secret. '*Domo arigato arimasu, Kano San,*' as they say in Japanese.

Very soon, we started forcing the changes in the conversations the team was having with project teams, what they were looking for and what the project teams should be measuring and delivering. It was not any more about complying with some standards that defined how the work ought to be performed, but it was about using complex statistical tools to *analyse actual performance* and developing mathematical models to predict the future.

More importantly, we started presenting data analysis using six sigma tools in various management reviews, and it was making a big splash. Infosys executives had never seen such analysis, and NRN was particularly pleased to see such reports. He had been demanding such data analysis for long, and he was very happy that I was providing them.

The most visible change was the slowly and steadily improving quality of the output, with the trend charts showing statistically significant improvements. This was very much in line with the core aspect of six sigma—what we measure always improves. This pleased NRN more.

He started reducing the Saturday brunch meetings, and very soon, he gained so much confidence in our progress that he pretty much cancelled them altogether. Nandan started smiling at me, and I was feeling pretty good about that.

Building on the initial success, we introduced a 'product quality' focus in addition to process compliance. Our attempt was to change the mindset of people from service delivery to product delivery. Even though what Infosys offered to customers was indeed *IT service, the resultant was a 'product'—'application' was the industry term—that actually accomplished some specific things the way their customers expected.*

This was the paradigm shift I was trying to accomplish. Making a service organisation think and behave like a product organisation. As expected, many resisted this change. 'What is this product quality you are talking about? We are a services company, and we don't make products,' they argued with me.

I just bulldozed my way through and rolled out the product quality focus initiative.

We started mathematically defining the quality parameters of what those computer programs were doing, treating every computer program application as a product. It was now all about *how clearly they were written, how easy it was to change them when needed, how fast they operated when many users tried to use them, and so forth.*

For example, how quickly do the ATM machines in a bank dispense money when asked? When we walk up to any ATM machine, we don't realise that hundreds of customers like us could be using the machines across the city at the same time. This can potentially slow down the big computer in the bank's data centre and keep all of us waiting. Another situation that all of us understand very clearly is the Internet buffering in slow networks when we see endless circles on the screen.

The delivery excellence team created a predictive model, using very complex mathematical formulae that cleverly predicted how such machines would perform when overloaded. It was now possible to check that out and make corrections in the design of the software so that ultimate performance would meet the specifications. The engineers need not have to wait for final stage at the customer location to find that out and struggle under pressure to correct them. It was always more expensive to correct anything in the final stage—like trying to change a defective piston ring after assembling a car.

Our main argument was that too much of process focus could come in the way of achieving the end result. We joked that we could get certified to highest process level when we made a life vest with concrete, as long as we said that we would do so in the process statements. Never mind that people would drown wearing them. It was an unfair argument but made the point nevertheless.

NRN then did something that was very humbling for me. When the famous Indian business magazine *Business Today* came in to do an article on how he was transforming Infosys quality, he asked the reporter to feature me. I was interviewed and photographed in several poses. The magazine published the report with me in full-page photo. This gesture doubled my efforts to drive more changes.

We launched our own six sigma programme and trained the delivery excellence anchors as Master Black Belts. Those Master Black Belts went with full gusto, using six sigma tools in various projects with significant improvements that were now being noticed by clients.

The real import of Shibu's advice 'to be here if you wanted to be there' was becoming increasingly clear to me.

We were so buoyed by the success of six sigma programme, and decided to launch it across the entire organisation. In classical GE style, it was decided to start the training from the very top. We launched a one full-day six sigma training programme for the entire executive board and service line heads. It was an elevating experience to have the founders and senior executives of Infosys in one room as captive audience and *we junior folks actually training them!*

It was a testimony of the humility of those great men who sat for a full day as students and politely learnt from us. No wonder Infosys was a learning organisation!

Emboldened by this, we then threw open the six sigma training programme for a wider audience and announced a Green Belt programme, seeking nominations from all service lines. The only condition was that each of them should come in with a client-relevant business problem to solve. This was the typical flag-waving GE programme style, minus the flags.

At this point, we had to take it through the process group of the corporate quality function, and there was a problem. Our efforts to change the flavour of quality and transfer of ownership to delivery had the potential for muddying the waters. This had to be harmonised with the decades of efforts of corporate quality. The way the founders resolved that demonstrated the culture of Infosys.

The chief quality officer vigorously pointed out that our six sigma programme could potentially confuse the organisation if it was done as a parallel initiative. As per CMM guidelines, any process change needed to be approved by his software process group. But he was very nervous and unconvinced about it.

The man who resolved this was Dinesh. Yes, the same Dinesh whom I cautioned in my job interview about 'drowning in the pond' if he went by average depth. As this interaction evolved, I would get to see the true greatness of the founders of Infosys.

Dinesh promised to give me a patient hearing for half an hour over lunch. The deal was that I should convince him why we should do six sigma in Infosys; failing which the training programme would be cancelled. After all, based on global evaluation of applicable quality systems for IT services, they had concluded that math-based 'DMAIC' six sigma was more relevant for manufacturing organisations. Now I was trying to bring it in.

It was pretty obvious that I was being asked to shake the long-held conviction of one of the founders of a great company in just half an hour. 'What are you going to do, boss?' asked my worried team.

'Let us focus on the here and now,' I said, trying to reassure them. 'The end result will take care of itself.'

I was very clear in my mind; after all, I had faced similar challenges in GE, where very bright and aggressive engineers had resisted the introduction of six sigma in their global software development centre. I had used all my persuasion skills to lead the team in integrating six sigma with the CMM process, which eventually won accolades from even the Carnegie Mellon University that had authored the CMM model.

I was ready and roaring to go.

The lunch meeting was for just three of us— Dinesh, the corporate quality chief, and myself. I had taken a PowerPoint presentation to explain the six sigma for IT, and Dinesh was surprised at that. He was feeling awkward to be eating while I was standing up to make the presentation. He was such a gem of a man; he insisted I finish my lunch and then start talking, willing to extend the meeting duration for my sake.

'The fundamental problem of the CMM model developed by Carnegie Mellon University is that it assumes that all work is done under the same roof, and influencing the way people work would ensure the quality of output. That is why there is excessive emphasis on inspection regime as opposed to assurance regime.' I went straight for the jugular.

'In this globalised world, work is performed in multiple locations across the world, and the complexity of what the software programs are accomplishing has grown exponentially. In my view, the plain vanilla CMM model is not adequate. It is imperative to have a robust quantitative measurement, analysis, and predictive models as a toolbox,' I continued.

Dinesh knew all this. 'That is why level 4 and level 5 processes of the CMM model insist on quantitative techniques,' he interjected.

'True, but what do they insist on measuring?' I asked rhetorically and proceeded to answer myself. 'You can measure anything you want, including say how long you review codes, and be satisfied with the simplest of analysis. Will it result in better program performance? Can Internet users have pages load faster? Can credit card users swipe and leave in a jiffy?' I paused.

'No way. We need to define variables that represent the factors that are important for end-users, measure repetitively, and use statistical techniques to make them work better.' This was me trying to oversimplify to make a point.

This got the attention I was looking for. Dinesh was now listening to me intently. I explained the potential quantitative techniques one could use and drew him into back and forth arguments. I depicted the potential problem scenarios and made him select the statistical tools he may like to use.

'Would you like to use a framework that gave you all the tools you just now liked or a framework that doesn't insist on them?' I asked. Then I went on to explain how six sigma provided the rigour, process, stat tools, and analysis methods all packaged into one neat methodology.

'The beauty is that this docks seamlessly into the level 4 and level 5 processes that you mentioned, Dinesh,' I concluded and sat down. I had talked for well over an hour, that too after taking half an hour for lunch. It felt so good. It was truly nice of that gentleman to have listened so patiently to me.

There was a moment of pregnant silence. Then Dinesh broke into one of his large grins. 'I wish I had met you years back,' he said, his voice booming. 'We went all over visiting so many companies in the world in search of the right quality improvement method and decided that we did not need six sigma! Only to meet you and get to learn that it is actually so important. That too for free at my doorstep!' He thrust his large hand forward to shake my hands. He was all smiles, and so was I. The corporate quality chief was equally convinced by my arguments and was willing to adopt this.

'So can I go ahead and launch the training programme?' I just tried to make it clearer.

'No, you don't do that,' he said, and my heart sank.

'After all the heroic effort on my part and boisterous support from him, he is still saying no?' I thought. It was very disappointing.

'*No, you don't kick-start the programme, but I do!*' he was grinning large again. 'I have learnt something from you today, and it is only proper that I come and inaugurate the programme. May I?' he asked. This is what makes Infosys a great company. The founders were such rare individuals, rarer human beings full of humility that is matched only by their achievements. While they are aggressive, they are equally flexible. When they are opinionated, they are equally open-minded too. They are simple, as they are demanding.

Six sigma rolled on in Infosys, winding its way through its quality system, touching everything they did. Not as a flag-waving, big-bannered, and splashy initiative like it was done in GE. It was subdued, underplayed, and almost apologetic. But equally effective.

Everyone could see Jack Welch jumping out from the clouds and hitting anyone not doing six sigma in GE. In stark contrast, it was all quiet persuasion, almost making people feel guilty if they did not do it in Infosys. It was the influencing power of Shibu, unseen but always felt. Infosys always gave the look and feel of GE shorn of its visible aggression. Shibu was slowly emerging as the Jack Welch of Infosys.

As the programme churned out more and more successful projects, the software process group formally adopted it as their own programme. Six sigma became a part of the corporate quality suite.

Shibu was smiling on seeing what we could accomplish in a short span of one year. It was no longer about stopping the Saturday brunches with NRN, but it was more about setting new benchmarks and beating them. Infosys was doing things that many other companies could not even dream of. There was a cultural shift happening as well, ownership changing hands to operations, no more inspectors catching any missteps. Instead, they became partners of the delivery teams.

Shibu always got bolder after every success, as if he was always testing his own ability to envision something larger and strategise. 'What next for him?' I wondered, little realising that I should be worrying about what next for me. This became apparent in our next monthly practice heads meeting.

'I would like to turn the whole conventional wisdom upside down,' he started. 'It is the industry norm to have only sales team in the market and keep the practice heads where the software factory runs. We should turn this model on its head and move the practice heads to where the markets are, closer to customers. This will give them an opportunity to understand what the clients are looking for first-hand, rather than hearing it from the sales force second-hand. I would like all of you to move to US, Europe, and Asia,' he continued and looked at all of us.

Some were excited about it, but most were reluctant. They had been travelling all over the world for many years, wherever the projects took them. They were tired of the nomadic style, which is the curse for the consultants.

A few practice heads agreed and plans were made for them. How about me? After the resounding success of six sigma programme, I was like a hungry tiger looking for the next prey.

'We set sail to Boston,' he said and enjoyed the bewildered look on my face. 'After championing delivery excellence in India and changing the quality paradigm, let us now see how we can drive excellence in how we manage our clients. The account managers who deal with our clients day-to-day are our true brand ambassadors, and we don't have a formal mechanism to enable them or evaluate them. That is where we have the highest cost and the largest client leverage.'

It was amazing the way Shibu kept moving the goalpost as we progressed. He had promised me uncertainty and excitement in the transformation journey, and he was keeping his promise in all measure. He seemed tireless in inventing ways of making the company a learning organisation like GE. I could only think of Jack Welch who was always visible, energetic, and demanding change for the better. If Jack was audacious in saying, 'If it ain't broken fix it,' meaning we should not wait for things to fail, Shibu was the epitome of acting on it. He seemed always ready to tear down things and rebuild better.

At the same time, he had the uncanny ability to stay focused on the 'here and present' so that short-term success was not traded for some vague dream of a long term. The way they mastered that in Infosys was to view the long term as nothing but a sequence of short terms with possible inflections.

It made perfect sense and was a validation of asking us to 'be here if we wanted to be there'.

'This is a long-term transfer to America, and so you will have to think deep about your potential career moves as well as how you want to deal with your family,' he cautioned. This was sometime in April, and this posed a challenge. My daughter Aparna was just getting ready to go to engineering college, and my son Arvind was stepping into high school. With freshman year admission being over in America, it appeared impossible to have my daughter move with us. Added to that was the SAT, TOEFEL, GRE things that my daughter needed to tackle. Breaking into high school groups would be no easy matter for my son either.

That is where my wife Jayanthi proved her leadership qualities. In the turbulent short four months between April and August, she managed to wind up our household, get our daughter clear the SAT, TOEFEL, and GRE with flying colours, and prepare my son for this journey very successfully.

This remarkable feat let me have the mental space to travel to Boston, look around to fix an apartment, meet guidance counsellors in Boston University, and explore high school options while trying to figure out new role responsibilities.

As the fall season started breaking in Boston, we reached Logan International Airport. Very quickly we settled into a tiny apartment—River Oaks—in Neponset Street in the town of Canton.

Never did I anticipate that my life would turn and take me 9,000 miles to America when I took the fateful thirty-yard walk with Shibu to his office. Never did I reckon as I reached River Oaks that I was setting foot into an upheaval in life that would continue to swirl for well over a decade.

Comically enough, in the all the excitement of taking my family into the brave new world, I simply could not open the door of the apartment building as we all arrived for the first time; I kept drawing it towards me rather than pushing it in. My son and I darted to the backside of the building, and he correctly pushed the door open. It was so symbolic as my son continued to be the problem-solver, a friend and a guide to me. He did not appear to be a kid of thirteen to me; somehow I felt that I had known him for a very long time.

It may perhaps be due to the fact that my father died young, leaving me confused and without direction. Maybe I was looking to someone, anyone, to come forward to guide me. And no one came, until that day in America, when my son spiritedly leapt forward to the baggage belt in Boston Logan, telling me he will take care. And there again at Neponsset Street apartment building as I fumbled unable to open the door, with my family waiting outside to step into the American home for the first time.

My daughter? She was not just the apple of our eyes; she was a diamond in my mind. She was bright, multifaceted, and of strong character. She took all the world travel I did in her young stride and never complained about coping up. She was steadfast and avoided idle gossip with friends and any vain behaviour. Sometimes I was sacred for her and wanted her to just go and have some stupid fun like so many other girls of her age. Her focus, discipline, and ability to cut through the maze and get to the core were impressive. We would time and time again use her as our touchstone.

The first couple of years were a battle as we tried to make sense of the complex society, every aspect of life being defined and governed by law. The American ecosystem appeared to be a paradox by itself, being very freedom oriented and yet very regulation driven. A deeper look revealed that regulations addressed deviations; as long as everyone operated within the ambit of some covenants, they were free to do anything. This was a stark contrast to India, where there seemed to be very little government regulations on anything, and yet everything seemed restricted; chaos can never replace freedom.

This difference makes transition and assimilation very difficult for immigrants from south Asia. We were no exception and had to go through the roller coaster ride.

While this swirl of assimilation was buffeting our personal life, I had to contend with equally forceful disruptive forces in my job as well. Shibu had grandly declared that we would transform the account managers at client locations. 'Where do we begin and do what?' I mused.

The destination appeared deceptively clear to us; we just had to make the account managers as our true brand ambassadors. It was just that we did not know how to do that. The traditional approach would have been to just redefine their roles with some stiff targets to achieve, give them tough love, and enforce an unfriendly reward regime.

But then, Shibu always thought differently, and I always acted differently. For us both, the secret of success depended on getting clarity on where we were to start, before we were able to prescribe any solutions. Being *here* was most the important requirement for getting *there*.

With all-round pressure, criticism, and disbelief, we set out to our drawing board to systematically define the role expectations and identify the skills needed. We interviewed almost all the account managers and reviewed most of the top accounts. Our primary goal was to get a clear understanding the deficiency.

We then worked with our 'learning university' specialist to design what we called a 'skill ladder', a comprehensive string of stepping stones for the account managers to climb, as the demand on their skills escalate.

Infosys was, and continues to be, a true learning organisation. Pete Senge, the legendary learning organisations guru from MIT Sloan would have been proud of it. The core skill and differentiator Infosys offered to clients was learnability of its employees. All hiring decisions rest not only on the skills applicants bring but also on how good they are in learning new skills.

It was not difficult for me to understand why Infosys was so focused on building a learning organisation; what was difficult for me to get was why many of Infosys competitors failed to see this. Many of them were content with hiring engineers with lower costs in mind and not necessarily hiring the minds that could lower costs to clients. In the process, they were seen as foot soldiers, while clients always looked to Infosys as the next and better version of Accenture.

The Shibu twist was in enlisting the sales team as well in this learnability equation. He demanded that even the sales teams needed to constantly learn new technologies and the solutions we could craft around them. In his mind, 'selling' was more about demonstrating how relevant Infosys was for the client.

Reflecting his belief that account managers were the true brand ambassadors for Infosys, we branded the training programme as the 'ambassador' programme. We partnered with corporate quality and supplemented the skills training with detailed work instructions for account management. We named it as 'long horn' process, as it was developed in Texas, a state famous for its buffaloes with very long horns.

My role was to orchestrate all this as the lone ranger. It was all excitement and sheer madness rolled into one. The only authority anyone could give in any virtual organisation was board-level sponsorship, and it was given in full measure; the rest was all up to my influencing skills.

When your primary weapon is influencing skills rather than any direct authority, you take a different strategy, a different approach in team dynamics. I called it 'wind out of sail' model in which you don't quell debates or dissent, but rather let the team run its course and run out of steam. It was as if I became a shadow, which they could not punch however much they tried!

Anyone who could get an opportunity to challenge me did just that, and the meetings many times descended into chaos, startling the couple of local consultants we had hired. They remarked that it looked like the American Wild West was being played again right in front of them! Coming from Texans, and in Texas, it was not a small thing.

Several leaders, who were my well-wishers, pulled me aside and advised that I should bring a sense of control soon; there were concerns that Paddy Rao was sputtering out. 'That tiger from GE whom Shibu brought is now dead, unable to survive Infosys' was the refrain.

It did not bother me in the least. It was but natural that they did not understand the 'wind out of sail' concept. I was convinced that ownership of any radical change vested with the team and not with any function. Ownership without authority is no ownership at all, and so everyone in the team had a right to challenge me. Letting them have a free run was a demonstration of recognition of that authority.

I was very sure that very soon the team would go beyond mere challenging and assume leadership in driving that change. The best way to accelerate that pace was to aggravate the situation. I was very good in using conflicts as a means of creating congruence of ideas, and so I provided a stark contrast to what they were doing as the best way. It was perhaps counter-intuitive from the recognised change management practices, but being contrarian was my forte. The change management traditionalists would have advised me to follow a 'yes, but,' style. It was not for me, no!

And it worked. Very soon, the team came around to working with me, a couple of practice leaders took upon themselves the responsibility of driving acceptance, and all of a sudden, we were making rapid progress. Very soon, we had collectively developed the outlines of account management process and the team called it 'our practical process'.

'You really pulled a success out of a disaster situation. It was a true Indian rope trick!' remarked the consultants as we sat over the celebratory dinner, as they dealt with their steaks. 'It was not at all a magic. I was just *here, not worrying about getting anywhere* in a hurry,' I responded, tackling a single large baked potato, perhaps the only guest eating a potato in a steakhouse. This was not lost on them.

'You are one heck of a fella. You are different,' they said, laughing aloud.

We washed off the dinner with some drinks and dashed to the nearby movie hall to see a movie. The local business leader's secretary had arranged it for us. The American secretary was all excited and gushed, 'You must see this movie as it is about your country India. It is a great story about love and sacrifice of an Indian pair.'

We settled down in the comfortable large Texan chairs in the movie hall and waited—only to see the story unfold in Africa, in Sudan! No India! When we went back to the secretary the next day to complain about it, she was very surprised. 'I thought that Sudan was in India!' Sudan was in India indeed.

With the 'ambassador' and 'long horns' settled down and the 'skill ladder' lapped up, life was becoming calm again. It was becoming a routine, and I started relaxing. It proved to be just the calm before a storm.

One day in Boston office, Shibu walked into my room.

'Have you heard of Lewis and Clark?' he asked. Of course I had. Thomas Jefferson had purchased the large tracts of land from Napoleon Bonaparte in 1803 that added almost a million square miles to America. He was keen to survey, map, and find clear waterways to the Pacific Ocean. He had a hidden agenda too—that of establishing sovereignty over the native American Indians who were living west of Mississippi River and prevent European nations from encroaching on the newly bought territories. He commissioned Capt. Meriwether Lewis and Lt William Clark to undertake a risky and arduous expedition for accomplishing this. They set out from St Louis in 1804 and trudged along some two years to reach Fort Clatslop. This was in Oregon State, on the Pacific coast some 200 miles south-east of Seattle.

'Why was he talking about this?' I wondered.

'I want you to go to Seattle and build our engineering services business. You have done enough of preaching about how accounts are to be managed for growth, and it is time now to practise what you preached. So please get in touch with our engineering business leader and plan to assume that responsibility.' Typical of him to move my goalpost again.

Seattle was about 3,000 miles away by road from our home in Boston. My son was in high school, and my daughter was in Boston University doing her computer engineering; how could I think of disrupting them? My wife made yet another courageous decision to support my career move. She would stay back in Boston with the kids and I could go to Seattle in search of the ways to build business for Infosys.

She would be the invisible Sacagawea, the Shoshone Indian woman who guided and interpreted for Lewis and Clark as they struggled their way through the American Indian territories in the expedition. Their expedition started from St Louis, Missouri, and followed the Missouri River westwards crossing Kansas, Omaha, Iowa, Nebraska, and Dakota and descended the mountains via the Columbia River into Oregon State to touch the Pacific coast. They had to contend with the Indian nations of Omaha and Lakota. They were dependent on Sacagawea.

Keeping with modern times, my wife would guide me through wireless, staying in Boston. She would manage the blizzards and snowstorms of New England winter all alone, as she did the retinue of all soccer moms, picking up and dropping off kinds multiple times in a day.

With excitement and anxiety I arrived at Seattle to start my new journey. After scouting around a bit, I rented an apartment in the same street in Redmond where the world-famous Microsoft was located, just a couple of miles down south. It really felt good to have Bill Gates come to work in my street.

To my American friends who were curious about my family, I would joke that my wife and I lived in the same street but in different houses. After a few seconds of increasing their anxiety, I would say we lived at the two ends of the 3,000 miles long freeway Interstate I90, she in Boston and me in Seattle. There was always a relieved laugh after that.

This move launched me into a whirlwind of travels, a wanderlust that took me a million miles. I was travelling like the merchants of olden days, travelling across thirty different states of America and the provinces of Canada.

The thirty-yard walk that I took with Shibu in Bangalore was obviously not over yet.

IF YOU WANT TO BE ADMIRED,
CREATE A CONFLICT.

CHAPTER 7

❦

Thirty Yards Can Take You a Million Miles

The aerospace business was a promising segment in the engineering services unit in Infosys. As a unit focused on engineering software development, in a company full of commercial software developers, it enjoyed the respect of being unique. For some, of course, this unique position itself was the reason for making fun of them.

They were already working for the largest European aerospace OEM in a small way, having a few engineers work in the client location in UK. They were not writing Java codes or configuring an SAP module. I had an opportunity to change all that by firmly establishing Infosys as any other engineering development company.

The Seattle company was launching a programme to revolutionise civil aviation, and it provided a great opportunity for us to gain a foothold in that program. The hitch was that the client saw Infosys as a Java and database company and so they were not willing to give us an opportunity in the engineering field. They felt that Infosys should focus on doing just what they were good at.

We could not fault the client for holding this view entirely. Infosys had for long leveraged the opportunities gushing out of the Internet bubble in its quest for rapid growth. It was very comfortable with being called a Java company and often was even willing to refuse when other opportunities showed up.

Although the Internet bubble had burst, this brand image stuck on like a leech, and now we were facing the onerous task of rebranding ourselves to be accepted as an engineering services company.

But we had to create a sub-brand without diluting the main brand. After all, we were doing roaring business in America in the commercial segment and did not want that to be jeopardised by this quest. How do we do that? Which part of my experience should I leverage now? If our past experiences cannot be leveraged, it meant we had learnt nothing useful out of it. Reuse of experience is the best return one could give to the organisation that has invested in you.

This sent me brooding and looking back at the role I played to get the European company accept Infosys a year back. Was there some learning, some technique that I could borrow and deploy in Seattle? I relive that European experience in my mind.

It was a typical cold and rainy English day when I landed in the sand dune city in United Kingdom. Shibu had directed me meet their CTO and convince him that we were as good as anybody else in engineering services. They were not to worry about our Java company image.

This was a tall order considering we only had a few engineers helping them out under supervision. It was not any ordinary engineering company, but largest in

Europe, specialising in aerospace. What was our claim to fame in this most demanding field?

We had a team of structural design engineers who had designed complex machines used in the manufacturing industry. They were masters of the design and analysis tools that were also used in aerospace industry. With the launch of competing aircraft design programmes by European and American companies, engineering services business opportunities were exploding. To deepen the experience and skill levels, the business unit head hired consultants from the industry. They were aircraft design engineers, retired after a long service in the Indian aerospace industry. This was our claim to fame.

And with this, I had to win the client's mind share.

It was not as if the client was not aware of our limitations; they were. They had insisted that we send all the engineers to work under their direct supervision in their works as we did not have rich aircraft 'domain' experience. What impressed them was the hard work, sincerity, and ability to learn shown by Infosys engineers.

We did not want to do it that way. We were a managed services organisation, and the primary cost lever was 'offshoring', which provided tremendous value to our clients. The client was reluctant to allow this for a Java company that was always swearing by the process model CMM. In their minds CMM was not relevant in their industry; the aerospace quality standard AS9100 was the one they relied on.

This standard expected what any standard would—impose conditions that are not uniformly applicable for all vendors. It was not the standard's fault—it was evolved for the companies that were designing and manufacturing the entire plane and not for service organisations like ours that did a small portion of the tasks.

But this was scary enough for us at Infosys, as many were not familiar with it, *not having worked in the aircraft industry*. The Y2K problem and the Internet bubble were so massive and it played so long that almost everyone had become 'Java guys'. There was no life beyond Java. At least till the bubble burst.

But Infosys was a company that solved the problems of clients; it was not just a Java company. It did not matter if it was a Java problem or a parts design problem. Our life depended on learning the skills needed and solving the client's problem. It was much more than that; our *purpose of existence* was to solve their problems. We were not willing to baulk at this opportunity and concede that we could not do it.

But then, Shibu had not brought in *a tiger from GE,* the humble me, who had worked for a decade in the aerospace industry for nothing. Why not press him to the task?

Promptly I was dispatched to sort this out and get the client agree to take us as engineering services company. This meant that I had to make some reluctant internal folks to dance with us and then convince the client to do the same. Both were equally apprehensive and suspicious of each other.

How does one make a reluctant partner dance? The conventional wisdom says we get gentle and charming, but for how long can you cajole? Particularly if you *do not have that long* to convince? In my mind, confrontation and conflicts were game accelerators that could potentially reduce the time required to accomplish anything. The trick lies in knowing how to diffuse the conflict at the right time, pull back, and get the team to agree and smile. Wrecking the team spirit in the bargain did not help and was a risk nevertheless.

My mind searched for the conflict for the occasion, as it were. In my mind, I could see the problem in two different ways: either see ourselves as *non-complying to AS9100 or as not requiring AS9100*. The latter was so attractive as it would simply have the problem go away! This was a sure bet in creating a conflict—the client was not likely to agree.

So I declared that as a six sigma and CMM level 5 company, we did not need any AS9100 certification; we were actually overqualified to do the tasks being asked by the client. As good structural engineers, we had the technical skills; six sigma and CMM compliance ensured that we were the best in process standards. There was nothing more to be done!

This was a classical judo move of deflecting the strength of the opponent, effectively neutralising him. Our corporate quality guru was naturally shocked and would have none of this. He just could not collect himself to carry this message to the client. How does one go an aerospace company and say that we don't need to comply with an aerospace standard?

Me? I was so sure of what I was talking about. After all, I had worked in the aerospace industry for a decade in India and United Kingdom and so knew the needs of the industry. On top of it, I was a six sigma Champion from GE world and had led some path-breaking implementations. The way I could reduce a problem to exact relevance, to the *tasks we were to perform,* made me very confident that the client would buy my arguments.

No wonder Shibu dispatched me with full bottom line and risk ownership of convincing the client. So there I was in that sand dune city of United Kingdom. I had reached a day earlier to the big meeting day to rest and think of a strategy. My colleagues took me around the town. It was amazing to see large sand dunes and a pyramid at the centre of the town. It was as eerie as it was reassuring. A pyramid and a sand dune in a UK city? How more counter-intuitive could one get?

This appeared to be a good omen for what I was trying to do—*be counter-intuitive!* It was a welcome company for me who was feeling all *alone* in the conviction that we will meet the client's expectation. With increasing confidence, we retired to bed for a good night's sleep.

We got up early, at the crack of the dawn, drowned a large glass of orange juice and scones and drove down to meet the client. We were ushered into a large conference room to meet the chief technology officer and his team. After the pleasantries and the customary jokes about English weather were said, I opened my arguments.

I laid out an argument taking the entire design, manufacture, and assembly workflow for aircrafts, picking up the relevant portion for the kind of work Infosys could get, and rhetorically asked, 'What exactly is the purpose of any process standard including the AS9100 that you are insisting on?'

Having lived in the aircraft industry for decades, the chief technology officer quickly responded, 'In short and simple words, to control risk and assure quality.' He was both curious and irritated.

I followed this with a detailed exposition of Infosys quality system and the progress made in six sigma. Taking the relevant portions of AS9100 standard highlighted the congruence with our quality process. 'What this means is that all the applicable parts of AS9100 is already baked into Infosys quality standards and hence we are already compliant. There is no need for any new AS9100 certification, truly speaking. Not that we will not get ourselves certified over a period of time, but my submission is that *you don't have to wait to start working with us in a managed services model,*' I declared triumphantly and sat down.

This was a very logical exposition of our position, and it made a lot of sense for the client's team. 'This is good logic. We will visit you in Bangalore for a five-day vendor evaluation audit. And if you come out successfully in the audit, our doors would open for you to set up a large offshore facility with hundreds of engineers working for our projects in a managed services model. Of course, we do expect that you will get certified to AS9100 standard in a couple of years.'

This was the outcome we wanted, and I was very pleased at the breakthrough. So were my bosses in Bangalore as I briefed them and advised the engineering team to get ready for the audit. This was received with mixed feelings. Many felt that we were sure to fail, and the responsibility was once again given to me to lead us to victory in the audit.

My strategy was to be just ourselves as that was the corner stone of my argument. 'Just be yourselves and do what you do every day. The secret of winning is not to attempt to win, but rather be ourselves and just do what we normally do. Winning is a by-product and never an objective.' This pep talk was very reassuring for the team, and they just went about as if there was not going to be any audit at all.

What happened during that week-long evaluation was nerve-racking, as the audit team was extremely thorough and demanding. They knew their job well and did not hesitate in demonstrating that. I kept assuring our team that we should not get overtly anxious, as it was sure to affect our performance.

The week-long evaluation was over, and it was time to know how well we had done. We assembled in JRD Tata Hall, our management review hall, to hear the closing remarks of the chief technology officer. The whole assembly broke into rapturous applause as he declared that we had passed the evaluation with flying colours. What he said as concluding remarks truly vindicated the stand I had taken all along.

'I must admit I am really ashamed of myself to have thought it necessary to audit Infosys,' he said in a typical roundabout British way. 'We saw so many impressive practices here that we should be actually learning from you. I will be very honoured to recommend to my management that we approve Infosys as engineering design partner of choice.' He stepped aside and proffered his hand to Shibu.

That started a great partnership that lasted several years with hundreds of Infosys engineers working hard to have their new large passenger plane designed and shake the world.

As these thoughts faded away, I stared out of the window of my office. Seattle presented its usual dark grey sky with intermittent drizzle, same as it was in England. It looked as though nothing had changed even after a few years and 1,000 of miles. The problem and weather were the same!

'How can I leverage the European experience to get into this American icon aircraft OEM?' I wondered again?

Though it was fashionable to ask rhetorical questions like 'What would Bill Gates do?', there was no way one could dart to his high-tech home in Mercer Island and ask him. So I decided to ask that to the lowly me—'What would you do, Paddy?'

'Create a conflict,' my inner voice commanded. 'There is no way you can plead your way through when they are not even willing to look at you as an engineering company.' This was interesting.

Conflicts can be very useful as they sharpen the focus of human emotions and thought process if managed properly. We can cleverly shift the focus to our point of view.

But then, what was the point of view that would change the mind of the client? It could not be a general sales approach, which was going on in any way without much result. The client had started a global hunt for selecting vendors to work together as a single global design team. With enormous difficulty I had gotten Infosys included in their itinerary for a vendor evaluation. There had to be something else that would give me an opening to catapult Infosys at the top of the heap. What would that be?

As I kept interacting with our engineers back in India to prepare for the client's visit, it dawned on me that my 'conflict' needed to begin at home with our own team, as they appeared to be taking this as a run-of-the-mill sales pursuit. A conflict was called for with our own teams in India to bring out a sharp message that could capture the imagination of the client.

What was wrong with our team? Being a conservative company, being very mindful of potential risk was a tradition. True to that tradition, Team Bangalore was preparing a defensive strategy, seeking a small participation from the client. It was the usual 'playing humble' routine, while this client was looking for a bold statement that would convince him to view Infosys as being more than just a Java company.

The defensive strategy would certainly play well into the hands of the sourcing team that felt we were not up to the mark anyway. We were, after all, a Java company in their minds, and our small play would confirm it. This thought was bothering me all through my flight to India, and by the time I landed in Bangalore, I had an action plan in mind.

I arrived in Bangalore a couple of days before the client's sourcing team to review the preparation, and the team made their pitch to me. As strategised, I promptly rejected the presentation outright. The team was aghast to see their two weeks of hard work being literally thrown into the scrap basket. It was clear to me that they had not taken my criticism from Seattle seriously.

Now they got to see my ability to start a conflict in full power. 'What exactly do you want us to do?' asked the business head in exasperation. 'The team has brought out all the skills story, case studies, and accomplishments as you had wanted, and yet you are rejecting this at such a late hour. We now have only the weekend in front of us to make any changes before the client arrives. Don't expect us to make any major changes as we just don't have any time left.'

'I don't want to tell the clients what we have done in order to establish our credibility. That is what they will be looking to hear and that is what every other potential vendor like us would do. I just don't want to do that,' I retorted.

'You don't want to establish any credibility?' he said incredulously. He followed it with an indignant 'Is it not what we do in such visits? You have been bombarding us that the client is viewing us as a Java company and so we have our story built around our aircraft design capability, and yet to refuse to accept. I just don't know if you are serious.'

The entire team was on me, now that they had the business leader backing them up.

'No, I don't want to establish any credibility. Rather, I want to challenge *their credibility* in launching such a global design programme of a game-changing airplane,' I said firmly. No wonder the meeting soon descended into bedlam with everyone piling up on me. They just could not digest the view that we could challenge the credibility of the client, particularly when our own credibility was in doubt.

'Don't you think it will be like attempting a suicide? What if the client turns the table on us and asks us to tell how this programme should be run? I never heard of a method of looking credible without establishing credibility!' The business leader was looking really worried. Though he always trusted my ability, he was not sure now where I was going with that approach. My entire approach seemed crazy at the minimum.

'Precisely,' I thundered. 'I want the client to take the bait and ask me the very same question. Here is what we should do to choreograph that. We will not start our presentation with the typical song and dance about Infosys credentials. Instead, we will start by saying how their new plane has to be designed by a global team and how Infosys will be able to contribute meaningfully. This will be provocative and the client will be eager to challenge us on our credibility. We then share our case studies with a very strong connect with our suggested approach. We then conclude that *they need us more than us needing their business.*'

There was total silence as the team and the business leader digested this. 'This way, the entire conversation will be about the client, his new programme, and relevance of Infosys in that context. It will not be about beseeching a client to *buy what we have,*' I concluded, and the team were now all nodding their heads. 'And, oh, by the way, none of your preparations are wasted. This is just shifting the context and sequence of messaging,' I continued, dramatically pulling out the sheets of paper out of the waste paper basket.

The team were now more than persuaded, and they went back to work to make the changes. 'Your conflicts are always useful but very tiring,' said the leader. I just smiled and walked away.

The client team arrived on Monday, and we moved as planned. Things happened as anticipated. The sourcing team was taken aback by the audacity of our pitching. Our team had gone way ahead of my advice and had even included a photograph of a big building with the client's name on it! There was a big laugh.

The chief technology officer and the chief information officer were very impressed and pleased.

The team's visit to our development stations, conversations, and discussions went very well, and they went back to Seattle, leaving a hopeful mood amongst us.

I recognised that the game was not over yet. 'It ain't over until it is over' as they say in America. After all, the sourcing team would have gone to so many other vendors after visiting us, and why would they select Infosys? Creating a feeling of satisfaction does not win deals; a feeling of differentiation does. While I had won the conflict with my team, the conflict with the client was yet to start. It was supposed to etch a differentiated image about us *before* the vendor selection was announced.

What should be my conflict with the client to clinch the deal? I kept thinking deep and hard, looking for a point of view that would be *unique* for us, *needed* by the client, and *unavailable* with the client.

As it happens always, an idea sprang up in the most unexpected place. While Archimedes had his idea in a small bathtub filled with water, mine flashed on much bigger platform on water. I was driving to work on the '520 Floating bridge' in Seattle, the world's longest pontoon bridge—a three-mile bridge floating on water, connecting Redmond with Seattle. As I sped away on the bridge, it occurred to me that I should take the most important aspect of the new plane, establish that they were weak in that, and insist that we were the best to help out. This would be audacious and a game changer if we could pull it off.

This definitely had plenty of scope for conflict; I could even be laughed at and thrown out forever.

In the famous Chinese treatise *The Art of War*, the celebrated strategist General Sun Tzu says that if we know ourselves and the opponent, we need not fear the results of a hundred battles. So I set out to identify the game changer that would define the client and us.

One of the earliest lessons I had learnt was that to be a successful manager, one needs to be aware of the environment in which one is operating. I followed this to a tee and always kept myself updated on the relentless innovation that was happening in Infosys.

The client was designing the most fuel-efficient plane and was planning to use carbon composites. I affectionately called them 'angel material', as they were very light but enormously strong. The material could stop a bullet and yet was light enough to be worn as a vest. It could carry a ton of weight effortlessly. My market intelligence fed me the great news that the client needed help in this very badly.

Infosys had acquired and expanded the team that had developed the tool for designing critical structural parts using composites. The engineers in that team had done pioneering work that was the envy of the world. It was believed that even Europe and America were behind when compared to their accomplishments. I tried to learn more about it during my Bangalore visits, but the team was reticent in sharing the details. The team had bright scientists, while the humble me was just a failed-physicist-turned-salesman. No wonder they felt reticent.

A conflict was called for to get them opened up. I triggered them by commenting that they were sitting in an ivory tower, in a cocoon, and it was time they did something commercially viable. This set them off so much that they drowned me with all the technical details, and I had to beat a hasty retreat.

Running away from brainy scientists was an old habit of mine, and it came in very handy.

But this experience gave me a clear idea of what we were capable of, particularly what our competition was *not* capable of. 'This will be my point of conflict with my client,' I told myself.

It bothered me a bit, though, to claim that our composite tool bench was the best. It was one thing to feel proud of yourself within the confines of your office; it was entirely another to go and claim that to the pioneer aircraft OEM of the world. We needed to do something better than that. We needed to have some reputed and independent body vouch for that claim. Which one could that be?

'How about MIT?' I told myself. That would be a coup. Who would ever dare to challenge an endorsement from the MIT, the Mecca of technology institutions? That would be it, I decided and flew down to Boston to meet the top professors at MIT to seek their endorsement.

Walking through the infinite corridors of MIT, I was wondering on how to convince them to endorse our workbench. I would be talking to the scientists who were probably one step away from the Nobel Prize. But all my experience of chasing Einstein in my college days as an amateur quantum theorist helped. If I had felt intimidated by their intellectual horsepower, it was barely so, and more importantly, I did not show it.

At the end of a tense week of meeting several of the MIT professors, I was able to zero in on the professor who was a specialist in the carbon fibre composites, and naturally, he was being consulted by leading aerospace companies of the world. I opened my laptop to give him an introduction to our composite tool bench; he stopped me.

'I know everything about your product,' he said in an irritated voice. 'I have been following the evolution of this product for quite some time. I always considered this to be the best in the market today. I have been expecting you folks to walk into my office for quite some time. What took you so long?' This was very encouraging, and here he was declaring our tool to be the best, even before I was seeking it. What he said next was a mood spoiler.

'But you guys are very late. I have been engaged by your European competitor already to develop something that will catch up with you guys. So I just can't help you,' he said, shaking his head vigorously as if he was chiding a rogue child.

I was stunned to hear that and felt a bit sad at the opportunity we had lost. But I was willing to push my luck. 'Can you at least give an opinion about our workbench, Professor?' I ventured. 'No harm in asking' was the best sales tool a hunter always carried.

'Unsolicited, no, I cannot do that according to my consulting contract with the other company. But if your client were to ask me, I am allowed to give my academic appraisal. But let me warn you fellas, your competition is hot on your heels and you only have a few months of advantage. Make the most of this lead before it vanishes.' The professor was nice, pragmatic, and business-like.

This was good enough for me to forge ahead and make my audacious claim to my client, which I did.

'Your goal of designing the most fuel-efficient plane cannot be met without help from Infosys, as we have the best composites workbench in the world.'

The client was scandalised to see a 'Java company' that had never made an airplane have the temerity to make such claims, instead of begging for an opportunity to participate in such a prestigious project.

'Composites workbench? We have hundreds of them hiding in so many computers. Our designers always like to develop their own tools. What is so great that you have one too?' protested the chief engineer.

'You are right in saying that your engineers have their own composites tool, but what we have is the world's best. If you have any doubt about my claim, you are more than welcome to seek an independent opinion from MIT. We can bring in the specialist professor who can share his unbiased evaluation,' I countered. This was something; he straightened up in his chair and let me talk further.

'There is yet another problem you have. *You don't know what all you know.* Like you rightly say, every designer wants to be innovative, do their own thing, spending money and effort. But they don't share their knowledge and output with anyone else. You folks must be wasting millions of dollars reinventing the wheel so often, you must be a bigger wheel company than Firestones.' I tried some humour. 'What you need is a definition and implementation of a knowledge environment that promotes innovation and sharing of knowledge accumulated. We will be happy to set up a knowledge lab for that,' I concluded.

This dual thrust of offering the world's best composites workbench and knowledge labs reverberated through the client's organisation, and the shock waves were heard at the very top. This set off a series of conflicts at several different levels, and we had to pass through some very tense evaluations and demos before we came out a victor. After a month's meetings, evaluations, and debates, the client made the final decision of selecting three vendors.

Infosys was at the top of the list. I seemed to have successfully created conflicts and won them all. This led to a business of hundreds of millions of dollars over the years.

While we had gotten the client on our side, having our teams to work on making the knowledge labs a reality was becoming a tall order. We had so many path-breaking ideas embedded in the architecture that our technical specialists felt I had committed something impossible. Gradually, I was getting sucked into the eye of the storm and getting crushed by the naysayers.

I had to become a 'pencil man' to break their mental blocks. The best way to conquer a team is to conquer the leader. So, I decided to take on the chief architect and convince him. We got ourselves locked up in a room and kept arguing for hours without any resolution. His fundamental objection was that the idea behind the knowledge labs was more philosophical than engineering and, therefore, was not implementable. Any amount of argument that everything begins with an idea did not cut ice with that pragmatic engineer.

I had to do something radical to break his reluctance and decided to take recourse of behavioural science. This branch of science helps us to understand how people behave in a particular way and provides the means of changing that.

The tool I was planning to use to bring about a change in him was a pencil. Just a pencil.

Chief Architect Ram lived in Los Angeles. He was doing a typical consultant's flight path—flying in every Monday into Seattle and getting back on Thursday evening. Before he left for Los Angeles that Thursday, I called him into my office and asked him to try out a simple experiment over the weekend at home, before he formally declined to implement knowledge labs.

'Can you do this for me, Ram?' I beseeched him. 'Just tell me how many different ways you can use a simple pencil.' He stared at the pencil I was holding, and not finding it serious, he ignored me. 'I am not trying to be funny, Ram. Just try it,' I persisted.

'Maybe a couple of different ways,' he said to brush me off.

'You can identify at least 100 different applications if you think hard enough. Here is what I suggest you do when you get home. Involve your family in this game. As soon as you get home, leave this pencil on the kitchen table, keep a sheet pad, and announce that all of you have to collectively identify at least 100 uses of the pencil by Sunday evening. And bring me the list on Monday. If the list has less than 100 uses, I will let you off the project. Is this a deal?' He was obviously in a hurry to get to the airport, and just to shut me off, he agreed to do so. He picked up the pencil and left.

Monday dawned, and I waited for him to show up. He walked haltingly into my office, and I tried to read his face, feeling a bit nervous myself. With a calm and emotionless face that all geeks have, he threw down the notepad on my desk and remarked, 'Sorry, Boss, I could not identify 100 uses of a pencil.' My heart sank.

'We discovered 150! Tell me when do I start my work!' He was all excitement. I just smiled and said that he could start right away. He just needed a provocation from an unconnected source for his mental block to be removed. The humble pencil did just that. Ram took such a great lead and personal interest in getting the knowledge labs implemented.

We went on to achieve several things that deepened and broadened our participation in multiple business lines of the client. They had operations all over America, and I was a common visitor to all of them. This made me some sort of a prospector of the gold rush times, taking me across the Mississippi; the tornado alley states of Texas, Kansas, Oklahoma, Illinois, Missouri; mile-high plateaus of Colorado, badlands, or the vast plains of Wyoming. So many peoples, so many cultures in the melting pot we called America.

The change was in air as we kept growing. Running a steady-state operation was not something I liked to do; nor did my managers want me to do that. The command for change came all of a sudden in a strange place in a strange situation, in Wichita, Kansas, while I was waiting to meet a client.

'Are you from India?' asked a sweet voice, and I spun back to see who was asking. I was waiting to get my visitor's badge at the reception of a large engineering company in Wichita, Kansas. There was a short American woman sitting quietly in a corner with her face almost covered by the large hat she was wearing.

'Yes, I am.' I was curious why she was asking me and was a bit embarrassed to hear what she said next. 'Can I shake hands with you?'

'Of course you could, although I am not a celebrity,' I said with false modesty and full curiosity.

'I am a Cherokee American Indian, native population of this country. We lost our war with the invading Europeans and lost all our lands to the settlers. Today I am waiting to rejoin this factory, getting back the job from which I was laid off a year back. We were happy for hundreds of years riding horses, hunting buffaloes, and without any notion of land ownership or boundary. Now we are either factory workers, or live a difficult life in a reservation,' she explained with a twinge of sorrow.

'I am glad to meet you too, but why do you want to shake my hand? I am not a celebrity,' I repeated politely as I held out my hand to her. I had been reading the tragic history of Native Americans and was very moved by her gesture. In my various travels across America, I always made it a point to visit paces of relevance to their struggle. King Philip's wars, the Trail of Tears, Little Bighorn, Wounded Knee, all swarmed in my mind in an instant, and I looked at her with a heavy heart.

'We are happy to see you Asian Indians prosper in America. We believe you and us are from same father, and to see you being so successful in America is heart-warming for us. It is as if we are getting our due back,' she concluded.

I shook her hands with all the warmth that could be mustered and wished her all the success.

My cell phone was ringing incessantly, and I had to pick it up, although there was a big caution asking visitors not to use cell phones. Shibulal was calling me from India.

'Can you go to Canada as country head? We have not been able to do very well there and are counting on you to revive our market in a short time. Can you do your magic?' he asked.

'Of course, I can. When do you want me to get there Shibu?'

'Next Monday, if possible.' This was typical as well. I finished my meeting in Wichita and flew back to my family in Boston.

All through the flight, I kept mulling over the last few years' journey and struggle to grow the business: countless meetings with clients, wins, and occasional defeats. The air hostesses serving tea and cookies exchanged meaningful glances as they saw me chuckling and almost talking to myself. I was thinking of the director who liked my 'conflicts-based team transformation model' so much that he even wrote down the functional equation I jokingly derived on his white board. It was a mantra for him to recite every day before he started any serious meeting.

A great satisfaction settled down in my stomach as I recalled that the CIO, who spent a couple of billion dollars, would grant meetings only if I was present. 'You bring a new perspective which I like, Paddy,' he would say. 'You don't hesitate to push a contra opinion and are almost always ready to pick an argument. Why would I spend my precious time to meet folks who tell me what I already knew? Meeting you has always been worth its time in gold.'

'Will this conflicts model work in Canada?' I asked myself and did not get an answer. Canadians were portrayed to be always very polite, gentlemanly. They were not great fans of what they termed as 'American style of shooting from the hip'. I had never been to Canada and had little or no understanding of the Canadian market. Other than feeling that I will find a way, I had no clarity on the strategy I would have to adapt a lot to succeed there.

I reached home and broke the news to my family, and they were very excited about me being promoted as a country head. Congratulatory messages started pouring in from my colleagues. Almost all the senior executives sent in best wishes except one—CEO Nandan, the 'no brunches please' man.

Weeks later when I met him, he pointedly asked if I had noticed that he had not sent the customary congratulations. Seeing me nod my head, he said, 'What is the point of sending all the good messages when one after another leaders have failed to grow the market? I don't know what Shibu sees in you, but what I know is that most of our business leaders in the US don't see a market in Canada. What magic are you going to do?'

'When would you recognise that I have succeeded?' I asked without directly answering him. He gave a typical Nandan response that makes a point succinctly. 'If you win a single contract valued at least five times your current annual revenue, I will pat you on the back.'

I agreed with him that we had no reason to exist if we did not grow dramatically.

'Mind you, I will give you only six months' time to do that,' he said brusquely, emphasising the last ounce of patience he had on that issue.

I flew into Toronto on a Monday afternoon and drove down to our office to assume the leadership role for the Canadian unit. The entire management team was assembled there with nervousness. They were as eager as Nandan to know what I would do differently to accelerate the growth that had eluded my predecessors for almost five years.

My answer to them was just two words—'boots' and 'mind'. They appeared disappointed that I was not sharing a complex and fancy strategy presentation with them.

'We are here to build a revenue engine that can deliver ten times the current annual run rate, and we are going to build it in three years,' I declared in the meeting.

They looked puzzled and almost every face was silently asking me, 'With just those two words?' I just smiled and ended the meeting.

One after another, the well-meaning folks trooped into my office, trying to educate me on how different the Canadian market was from the US market and what we should be doing. By the time the week was over, I had received so many contradicting bits of advice that cancelled one another. We would be doing nothing had I listened to all of that.

The 'boots and minds' was an oversimplified statement of a deeper strategy arrived at after a careful evaluation of what was going on in our Canadian business unit. It was my conclusion that the unit was given a secondary importance by the US-based business leaders as the Canadian economy was less than one-tenth of US economy. Hence it did not capture the mind share of leadership with sales folks trooping in from the United States whenever they could. The Canadian clients resented this. The visiting salesmen from the United States did not possess the deep understanding of the Canadian way of doing business at all, and it did not help either.

But then, did I myself comply with the 'the boot and minds' requirement? Not really, considering I was myself new to Canada and hence did not have any idea about the market. Perhaps the 'mind'? Indeed, reviving Canadian business was the only responsibility assigned to me, and I was not going to throw away my credibility by failing.

Like it happens always, there were a couple of managers who had excellent grip on the Canadian market, but for unfathomable reasons, they were not given the prime mover positions. Andrew and Sesh became my trusted lieutenants, my conscience keepers. They were Canadian nationals who had spent several years working for various clients and had deep first-hand knowledge of what the Canadian clients' expectations were. More importantly, they knew exactly what the clients *did not want to see from us*.

There were initial moments of mutual anxiety as we sized up each other. Once we got that phase behind us, we bonded as one team. For them, I represented a confusing picture; I projected an American style, Indian mind, and a Canadian outlook. It did not help matters at all that I was so critical of everything Canadian, but they were gratified by my unwavering commitment to the success of Canadian operations.

They were very honest people, and sensing my open forthright style, they candidly opined that I should stick to strategy and leave the actual sales process to them. This was a very reasonable demand, and I had no hesitation in acquiescing to them. After all, they knew the Canadian market like the back of their palms. In addition, Andrew was a master strategist while Sesh was a master of delivery operations.

Much later, after multiple large wins, they would share the apprehension they had on interacting with me more openly—they could not let a 'shoot from the hip', 'take no prisoner', 'Dubhya' (that was how President George W was affectionately called) fan loose on to peacenik Canadians.

We three started putting together a large team of local Canadian sales force, replacing the US-based sales team. This took me on a collision course with my fellow US colleagues as well as our corporate finance that felt I was throwing good money after bad. Everyone expected me to fail and was mentally planning to draw the shutters down on us. My game plan of increasing the investments was at loggerheads with what they were trying do.

But my accepting the challenge from Nandan to win a single contract ten times our annual revenue acted as a shield for me. It got me the investment we asked for. The CFO was perhaps indulging me as they would with a death row inmate's last meal!

My conviction was that the local sales force brought in not only local connect and market knowledge but also their commitment to live or die with the market. It was not an add-on job they were doing.

My focus next shifted towards the Canadian CIOs to get them excited about Infosys. In their minds, we were not giving them the due importance, and some of them even refused to meet me. A couple of them were open enough to ask me to seek an appointment a year later, should I still be in Canada! These statements confirmed my hunch on where the problem was.

We had a bad history with most of the clients there, and to start with, there were only a limited number of 'Fortune 500' clients there. They were definitely not in a hurry to get back to business with us after having had an unpleasant experience with us in the past.

A regular, classical sales process was not going to break the ice again. This meant, I had to concoct an unorthodox approach, which I very soon did. The new market expansion strategy had three components—first geographic, second deal size, and third service type. The traditional process would mean you try to be geographically closer to where you operate, start small, and play on your strength.

I decided to turn this upside down and go for clients on Canadian west coast in provinces like British Columbia, Alberta, Manitoba, and Saskatchewan. Further, I directed our sales team to bid for large multimillion-dollar multi-year deals, i.e. aim big. Finally, I asked them to pitch for services that Infosys had started of late and so did not have a bad history.

I christened it 'non-Euclidian strategy' and started reaching out the CIOs with gusto. Very soon, our sales force was getting energised, and now we had our own Canadian 'Westward, Ho!' in full swing. On the internal side, we launched a blizzard of communication, reporting every meeting with clients, much to the amusement and ridicule of everyone else. 'This week's flash news? Team Canada had a lunch meeting!' they joked among themselves.

My idea was to create a splash to ensure that we remained in the limelight. My lieutenants Andrew and Sesh complained that while *I was creating a splash, the ridicule they faced was actually wetting them.*

In the great churn that followed, we slowly started winning deals. It started as a trickle of small deals that kept growing and growing, and in the sixth month, we announced a 'Nandan Deal'—a single contract that was five times the size of our annual revenue. Sesh won it for us from a client in western Canada. His dedication, perseverance, and eye for details won it for us. True to his word, Nandan called and congratulated me, remarking that I had virtually saved the unit from closure.

In another six months, Andrew got us another deal that was *ten times* the base year annual revenue. It matched his style of strategic thinking, aligning with and complementing the client CEO's market expansion.

Andrew and Sesh kept winning, and we were on a roll. In three years, *our annual revenue was ten times* what we had in the baseline year.

We were getting noticed by everyone. Analysts interviewed me and were taken aback when I declared that the addressable market segment open to us was a billion dollars. They promptly ignored it and did not print it. The chamber of commerce invited me for a talk in which I took the Canadians to task for thinking small and missing their rightful position on the world stage. Provincial ministers wanted to meet us, and I cautioned them that Canada would be dropping below the BRIC countries if they remained inward focused. There were podcasts, news items, and the usual stuff that happens when you get successful.

Picking up admirers always happens, and that was not special. But when many admired not only the accomplishments but also the method adopted—*conflicts as means of differentiation*—it gave me a great sense of vindication.

This became some sort of a personal brand statement, following me like a shadow for a couple of decades. At every cusp of life, I used conflict as the means of gaining sharper focus, getting attention, garnering strength and support to win. It happened time and time again.

It permanently bonded me with the teams I led, battle-scarring them often, prized as decorations of valour by the admirers. Toil they did, suffer they did, angry with me they were; but they always came out with enhanced personalities and their lives were changed forever.

While many were celebrating all this, there was one man who went about with his life as if nothing had happened. It was Shibulal. If he was proud about our success, he did not show it. I understood why—*this success had happened already in his mind even before it occurred in reality*. As Sun Tzu's saying goes in *The Art of War*, '*Victorious warriors win first and then go to war*'.

Shibu was one hell of a victorious general. After all, it was his idea to send me on the rescue mission. It also meant that my tenure in Canada would be over soon and a new battle raging in his mind would come out alive.

Soon enough, a call came, asking me to meet him in Boston. I went across in full anticipation of some new command from him.

He just looked at me and smiled quizzically. I understood the meaning of that familiar smile. It only meant that something else was cooking in his head and he was indulgently allowing me to bask in the past glory for a while. I looked out of the window at the adjacent cemetery and saw a line of cars driving in a dignified single file, blinkers flashing. They were coming in to bury a dead man. 'A new journey would begin for him,' I thought and looked up at Shibu.

'He is perhaps cooking up another battle for me in his head, and it will come very soon,' I thought. He knew it, I knew it, but we both decided to pretend that the days of battles were over, never to return, and enjoy the peace. Both of us knew that generals who did not know to enjoy the peace would not know how to win battles.

'What will that new battle be?' I wondered. I did not have to wait far too long for that.

'We are trying to fundamentally alter how we work in America. Can you travel to New Jersey and meet with our America's head Ashok Vemuri? He will define your new battle.'

TO KNOW YOURSELF,
UNLEARN EVERYTHING.

CHAPTER 8

❧

Happiness Is Your Name

I sat down in the quiet car of the *Acela Express*, boarding the train in Route 128 station, and closed my eyes. I was on my way to New Jersey to meet Ashok and get to know of my new assignment. I always hated to drive down to New Jersey or New York from Boston; the interstate Highway I95 was invariably chock-a-block with traffic around Connecticut exits, and we ended up crawling. Why not take the flights? Well, post-9/11, no one wanted to waste three hours in security lines and traffic for an hour's flight. The train was the best option. Among trains, *Acela* was the best.

The high-speed train took three hours to reach Metropark station in New Jersey, it had Wi-Fi, pantry car, and a quiet car where cell phones were not allowed. One could log into Wi-Fi, surf, or work. It also gave enough time and opportunity to close the eyes, reminisce, sleep, and dream a bit in the quietude.

The fact that I would be meeting Ashok to hear of my next assignment made me a little apprehensive. How could a road warrior with three decades of experience get nervous? What is the meaning of an experience then? This thought made more nervous.

But I just remembered a medical research report I had read a few years back. A team of neuropsychologists was studying the behavioural pattern of experienced and rookie paratroopers once a mission was announced. One would expect the experienced paratroopers to take the announcement calmly, while the new ones were expected to panic on the announcement. But the study found the response to be surprisingly opposite.

They found out that the experienced paratroopers got tensed up as the horns blared and the mission was announced in the base camp. They, however, had the nerves of steel as they jumped into enemy territory even while facing a hail of bullets. The response of the rookies, on the other hand, was exactly reverse. The inexperienced were all bravado after the announcement until they reached the enemy lines. At that point of mission, the rookies were a bundle of nerves and had to be literally pushed off the aircraft.

On deeper analysis, the psychologists discovered that what conditioned the paratroopers was the aggregate response of the cumulative experience. The experienced knew what was likely to happen, having gone through the ordeal several times, with their body and mind starting to prepare the defensive mechanism. The new ones obviously did not have any experience to make them nervous.

This thought comforted me that nothing was wrong in being nervous, so I continued to be nervous. I knew that when the battle cry happened, I would be ready and calm and would act. I pushed the seat back into a reclining position and plugged in my Bose headphone. My favourite Mozart was waiting to play. Among his great compositions, the Requiem was my choice.

Why did I choose the Requiem at that time? A Requiem mass is usually conducted in Roman Catholic tradition to repose the soul of dead people. What made me select that composition? Whatever the reason was, the music was truly elevating. It was perhaps another paradox that music intended to repose the dead people's soul was actually elevating the living.

I sure was seeking paradox in everything!

I closed my eyes and started drifting into heaven. Why not? Mozart was seeking the heavenly father to forgive—'*Confutatis maledictis Flammis acribus addictis Voca me cum benedictis*'. I was so fond of this that I had read the meaning of this Latin song. 'When the accursed have been confounded and given over to flames, call me with the blessed.' Why did the meaning appear very appropriate for me at that moment?

Johannes Chrysostomus Wofgangus Theophilus Mozart was a prolific composer from Austria. A child prodigy, he composed some extra ordinary pieces in his short life of thirty-five years. He lived during the mid-eighteenth century.

Mozart started playing music from the age of six and could play multiple instruments. His father was perhaps a pushy man, driving Mozart endlessly, taking him on tours to display his talents. The young Mozart hated this, not wanting to be a 'performing monkey', and began composing his own masterpieces. He was prolific and composed sonatas, symphonies, masses, concertos, and operas. Sophistication and strong etching of emotions was his hallmark, and one could see it boldly manifested in his compositions.

There was a deep mystery behind the composition of the Requiem. The patron who commissioned that piece was a secret who held out the commission through an agent, never revealing his true identity till the end. Mozart was poor—having spent all his wealth in binges—very sick, and dying when he was commissioned to do this. He wanted the money so badly that he willingly subjected himself to being rushed by the agent. He worked very hard and was so exhausted by that experience; he started to feel that he was actually writing his own requiem. Even now many believe that he died without finishing it.

Maybe due to this personalisation, the Requiem turned out to be a great, moving, masterpiece. I descended into depths of the musical experience, started drowning in my thoughts, and soon became contemplative.

What exactly are we chasing in life? When all the waves of life run out, what do we gain? As I looked back reminiscing nearly fifty years of my life's journey, what struck me was the remarkable lack of real difference in my mind over the years. My emotional well-being and contentment appeared exactly the same that day in my train journey as it was when I accompanied my dead father to Chennai in a taxi, some five decades back.

The progression in age, status, wealth, and experience did not seem to have mattered at all. If nothing had changed in me notwithstanding dramatic changes in life, why was I chasing those things in life? What then was the purpose of all the travels and tribulations I faced?

Where did I arrive after travelling all the millions of miles across the world? I had no idea of what I brought with me into this world when I was born; I have no idea on what I will take with me when I die. What happens to the things we accumulate in this brief interregnum called life?

Mozart was not helping either. He seemed as conflicted and confused as I was. He continued his pathos, '*Lux aeterna luceat eis, Dominie, Requiem aeternam Dona eis Dominie*' (May eternal light shine on them O Lord, grant the dead eternal rest O Lord). What exactly is this eternal rest that all the religious and spiritual leaders talk about? How do we get it? It looked as though Mozart was convinced that the worldly accomplishments and possessions could not give us the eternal rest.

Do we get it just by begging the gods, who seem so elusive that no one ever gets to see? Or do we take control of our destiny and master all the things we ought to know? But what are the things that we ought to know?

No one ever knew, nor will ever know, what all is to be known, let alone know them. Are we condemned to wallow in this pitiable state of winning everything but gaining nothing?

As the enthralling music of Mozart's Requiem continued to uplift me into a contemplative mood, a long-forgotten face began to appear in my dream. The guru who rarely spoke to me smiled at me, this time also in silence.

'I taught you all the things you needed to know, my child,' he appeared to say. 'You seem to have forgotten all that. Let me tell you again. The best learning is to *unlearn things you already know*. What remains when everything is unlearnt is not emptiness, or vacuum, but bliss, eternal happiness. Happiness is your nature and so why search and lament?' He smiled and disappeared from the dream.

This thought wave shook me up. In all probability, the thoughts were bubbling out of my subconscious mind and manifested in my dream, talking through the form of my guru. I had been deeply, for quite some time, thinking over Kapila *Muni*'s Sankhya philosophy, enunciated some 3,000 years ago. The basic premise of the Sankhya system was that we were all a victim of our own mental models about the universe and ourselves. Consequently, the best way to become happy was to unwind all that.

I was getting increasingly convinced that the Sankhya hypothesis was very aligned with cognitive psychology and merited better scrutiny, and it seeped into my subconscious.

I perhaps tried to project this conviction on my guru in my dream. But then, I got deep into this Sankhya philosophy due to his putting me on that path any way. From time to time, he asked me to participate in group activities of some of his followers. I found the activities of those groups were so different from each other, it appeared to be random at that time. Some were ritualistic, some argued endlessly, some meditated, some were material scientists, some practised yoga, while some were contemplative. Such a participation all seemed pointless to me, even though I continued to follow the directive of my Guru.

Over a period of time, my understanding of the 3,000 years of philosophising in the Danube-Indus valleys improved. It was dawning on me that my guru was actually taking me through the demonstration of the 'six *darsanas*' or the six points of view that dominated classical Indian philosophical edifice. So I could not tell for sure if the guru appeared in my dream on his own or I made him appear. The whole thing appeared unreal.

This is another paradox we deal with—unreal concepts producing real results, making it difficult to decide if the unreal concepts were unreal after all.

Be that as it may, it set off a tsunami of recollections. I had spent decades trying to learn so many things at his behest. Now he was reminding me to try to unlearn them bit by bit? Why did he then nudge me to learn them in the first place?

What is this unlearning business and why unlearn? All the interactions I had had Umesh, my senior in college, started flooding into my mind. An accomplished yogi, he was kind enough to take a few of us along with him into the exciting world of self-discovery. The hundreds of hours we spent with him changed the very fibre of our existence. While we all started and parted at different levels, what was common was *we were all changed forever in life.*

Umesh took us to his guru, Abhinava Vidyatheertha at Sringeri, the ashram set up by the eighth-century philosopher Shankara. He was a scholar, philosopher, high priest, yogi, guru all rolled into one. He had the uncanny ability to be the person who was talking to him. Everyone felt he or she was being treated special by the guru. He spoke rarely with me but instructed me in full measure. He never enforced any regimen on me but helped me seek self-restraint. He never asked me for anything, but granted me everything that I needed.

Both Umesh and he helped us understand that we are the very definition of bliss, and there was no reason for us to be unhappy. The trouble was we did not know what to do with this understanding or how to integrate it with the normal life we were leading.

To make our life more challenging and yet interesting, the guru disbanded our group and sent us all to live our respective lives, chasing pleasure, wealth, name, and fame. We could never understand the reason why he took us on board first and then why he dispensed with us completely. We plunged into the vortex of mundane life nevertheless and got dispersed in various parts of the world. We were like beggars moving around in rags, seeking alms, not realising that there were diamonds hidden in the loincloths.

All but Umesh, who returned to his 'caves', spending the rest of his life in meditation and contemplation. I saw less and less of him over the years, *but he never left me.*

The mad diversity of experience I was thrown into was perhaps a training in itself. This 'Magellan-like' travel around the world brought me face-to-face with a variety of cultures and peoples. While they all looked and behaved differently, *I felt they were the same as an inner core* as I looked into their eyes. I simply could not feel any difference, and what was more, it felt as if they were actually me. The regional, racial, and cultural differences seemed just a matter of definition and meant so very little. It took several decades and some difficult experiences for me to understand the 'why' of that feeling.

Ignoring the diamonds in my loincloth, I kept busy, begging around, chasing pleasure and wealth. Driven by intellectual ego, I spent years reading hundreds of books, debating with anyone I could, fighting to establish my point of view.

Little did I realise that all points of views were totally irrelevant as they were just what they were, mere *points of views.* Likewise, every aspect of life is burdened by *our* definitions and hence is very subjective. They hold good only for us, that too in a specific context, and hence have a great potential to cause conflicts due to wrong judgments.

This leads us to a conclusion that it is almost impossible to *objectively* prove any one view as the best among the many possible views. Our trying to feel better than anyone else is as burdensome as it is to denigrate anyone else.

The best way to unburden ourselves and feel light is to dissolve all definitions. We have to start from the outside and dismantle all the definitions and biases; when we get to a point when no external definitions stand, we need to start *dismantling the definition of ourselves till nothing remains.* It is not an empty nothingness, but a rich nothingness that results when the 'subject, object, process trio' is dissolved. This nothingness is the greatest joy, a bliss that never leaves you, because you are the bliss. You 'left it' and now return to it.

This bliss could never be taken away from you, *as you are the bliss,* not as if you have the bliss. This bliss cannot be eroded, as *nothing can be taken out of nothingness.*

I was not alone in gaining an understanding of this puzzle, nor did I invent this. Scores of thinkers have thought about it over thousands of years. It took nearly 3,000 years for the great thinkers living between the rivers Danube and Indus to get it right. The irony of it all was that they spent so many years learning about themselves and others, only to discover in the end that what they should be actually doing was to unlearn.

The Vedic Aryans, Greeks, Persians, Egyptians, Sumerians spent gargantuan efforts to answer just three questions—Who am I? What is this Universe? And where do we go from here? Those riddles were so mystifying that several religions came out of them with a steady flow of gods and goddesses with attendant rituals. Countless animals were sacrificed to propitiate them and in return the gods took millions of human lives in various religious wars and associated disasters.

It never occurred to the followers of those gods to stop and ask themselves, how could purportedly a liberating principle cause so much misery and devastation? Nor did they pick up courage to come to terms with the answer and abandon the principle by dismantling the *acquired knowledge* about them. These gods and principles were not self-discovered but were handed to them by the prince and priest schema.

As the monarchs in Greece, Rome, and Persia amassed seas of armies to repetitively attack each other in their vain quest for greatness and land, philosophers tried to examine the very relevance of their existence. They came in hordes as counterweight to the egoism of kings.

Gotama, Yajnavalkya, Plato, Aristotle, Socrates, Zarathustra and the like searched themselves and gave the world an outpouring of complex thoughts and opinions. Repetitively they stressed that the entire search was misdirected. But no one listened.

The incessant debates I had in my mind with them took me nowhere. It was slowly becoming clear to me that *their battles with themselves and among themselves* appeared to be as futile as those of Cyurus or Alexander on various wars. No one won in any of his or her battles. There are never any victors in any war. I drifted away from Umesh and wandered in the world in search of personal glory, travelling from country to country, city to city, house to house for decades. I walked on the Great wall of China, searched the pagodas of Tokyo, and visited monasteries in Shanghai, blue waters of Male, and prairie of Wyoming but could not find what I was searching for. If we are the personification of bliss, how do we get it back? Is it something reserved for the Buddha living in isolated caves, or is it within the reach of ordinary mortals doing their daily battles of life? I was not willing to accept that it was only for the chosen ones.

The million miles of travel did not move me an inch forward. All the progress made in the fifty years of marathon had left me more troubled than ever. Philosophers like Plato and Yajnavalkya were not helping either.

Why should somebody dead for 1,000 years make sense to us? May be the living legends could teach a thing or two as they are around us in life and blood. They are not a figment of anyone's imagination and should be providing clues relevant to our times.

I kept looking for celebrities at airports to observe them and soon enough things began to happen. Psychologists are damn right in asserting that we get to see only what we seek.

It was 'The Little Master' Sunil Gavaskar at Bangalore airport one day. The best cricketer in the world, ever, was sitting all alone, as if he did not matter or even exist, and he looked happy for that. How did the great actor Kamal Hasan or maestro Ilayaraja behave at Frankfurt airport as we all waited for our connecting flights to America? Juts a weak smile at me, acknowledging my respectful looks, and they were just gone, as if they enjoyed their anonymity.

Or that smiling monk, who keeps declaring that his religion was kindness? No other passenger in that tiny plane even recognised that it was Dalai Lama with Richard Gere, sitting there quietly and enjoying himself.

What were those famous personalities demonstrating by their behaviour in public? They all seemed content and happy in being left alone, shedding their celebrity image. Were they the living proof that no accomplishments really mattered to anyone and so we need to drop them from our minds to find our peace?

My guru asking me to unlearn was beginning to make a great deal of sense. I started wondering in my half sleep if there were any stories around the importance of unlearning in our hoary past, and sure enough I recalled one—the story of Yajnavalkya.

Yajnavalkya and Uddalaka, the ancient gurus of the Vedic period, postulated that pure consciousness was the innermost core of human make-up. They assert that principle repetitively in Brihadaranyaka, Chandogya, and Svetasvathara Upanishads. In their view, this pure consciousness is of the nature of bliss, unattached and uninvolved. Instead of identifying ourselves with this, we attach ourselves to our ego-driven mind, and as a consequence, we suffer unhappiness. This was their premise. Of the two, Yjanavalkya had an interesting and revealing life.

Yajnavalkya was the legendary sage from Vedic India, very learned and scholarly. This made him very proud, and he started feeling that he was smarter than even his guru Vaishampayana. The guru got annoyed at this and wanted to teach him a lesson and so ordered him to vomit the acquired knowledge, ostensibly to show that he did not deserve it. Yajnavalkya obeyed the guru and vomited all his acquired knowledge. That knowledge was so precious even as a vomit that the other disciples took the form of partridge bird and ate it. The Sanskrit name for partridge is *Tittri* and hence the vomit eaten by the birds came to be called as Taittriya Yajur Veda.

This Yajnavalkya went away from his guru, deciding that he will not learn any more from another human being. A self-manifest knowledge cannot be demanded back. He went experimenting with his thoughts treating, the sun as his guru. The sun never questions any one nor abandons any one, any time.

In his ferocious pursuit of knowledge, he decided to leave his wealth to his two wives and retire to the forest. One of his wives, Maitreyi, was the wise one and she pointedly asked him if wealth could make her immortal. On being told that wealth was not a gateway for immortality, she sought the pathway to immortality. Yajnavalkya proudly decided to teach her all he knew about it.

Yajnavalkya continued his intellectual battles with many scholars and finally took what is gloriously called *Vidhwat Sanyasa* or knowledge-based renunciation and retired to the forest.

I saw this story differently as two very important things struck me pretty odd.

One, Yajnavalkya had to take *Vidhwat Sanyasa*, which in my mind was *renunciation of knowledge,* rather than renunciation based on knowledge. Considering that his guru demanded that he vomit all his knowledge once, it was more likely that he had to renounce his knowledge and get humble.

Second, when Maitreyi asked him if wealth could make her immortal, she probably knew the answer; one had to have the wisdom *even to ask such a question.* Maybe she was telling him, rather than asking him. Yajnavalkya simply did not get it; he was puffed with vain pride and went on to instruct her, while she really needed none.

No wonder he had to struggle for some more time, wasting time pursuing knowledge, until he renounced knowledge.

Like Maitreyi, my wife, who had been my permanent moral compass, ended my quest for me. While I was busy fighting with others to defeat their points of view, my wife went along partaking diverse views with all humility. While my mind was full of turbulent waves, she was a placid lake.

She was attending a congregation in our neighbourhood in Boston and offered to have me give a series of lectures at their congregation. She convinced them that I would bring a fresh perspective to their quest. She somehow believed that my being a renegade thinker will be helpful for the disciplined conformist congregation—or so I assumed. The congregation's coordinator Mouli came home to have a long conversation to define the perimeters of my talk.

He was actually evaluating me, and I vainly found it amusing.

They were very sincere, dedicated, accomplished folks, who lived almost a commune life, spending the free time together. They were very religious and devoted to worship in all its dimensions, proudly bringing up their kids in Indian tradition in faraway Boston. Their kids were very bright, well-rounded, and talented. Many of the kids were star singers and performers in Indian classical arts.

After a very long chat, Mouli was satisfied that I sure would bring some value and was more impressed with my comprehensive background. He prepared a flier providing a glimpse of my career progression, 'erudition', and my subsequent decision to throw all the books away as meaningless. The last piece caught everyone's attention, and they were all excited to hear me out.

Mouli and I agreed that we would name my talk series as 'Think Series'. After all, my core message was that people must think for themselves and find a way rather than forever seek guidance from various gurus.

Little did I realise that this would launch a five-year quest in which instead of me weaning them away from books and starting them to think, I would end up reading more books and start thinking differently. Life has a very funny way of getting at you.

The day of the first talk arrived at the home of a simple-minded pair, Mohan and Janaki. Their home was sort of a central node for most of *satsang*, congregation of the pure. True to my nature, I did something different, unexpected by almost all of them. I started the session with a prayer in the Wampanoag language, the tongue of the Native American Indians of that area in Boston. I had felt it fit to pray to the local spirit, rather than a god some thousands of miles away in India. I was also making a statement that praying to any god and in any language was equally relevant or irrelevant, as no one was sitting on a cloud dispensing special favours. This first session did not go very well at all.

They, nevertheless, participated with great zeal in all the following sessions, and we challenged each other all the way. While they were very polite and keen to listen to me, they were very sure of themselves, willing to move only slightly from their position. Similarly, while I was very open to being challenged (these were a 'think' session, weren't they?) and gave them infinite space to move around, I was set on my position like a rock. What was the purpose of such an interaction then?

My fundamental idea was to create a churn in the minds of people and *make them want to change*. No one ever changed anyone by advising from outside, without the willing participation of the concerned person. To gain participation, we need to create a commotion and disruption in the minds that would make the person yearn for change.

Over the years, many had told me of the famous English proverb: 'Ten men can take a horse to a pond, but not 10,000 make it drink'. In my view, we did not need 10,000 to make it drink but *just one would do*—the one who knew how to make the horse thirsty. *The horse would run on its own to the pond and drink by itself.* This was what I was trying to do in that Norfolk *satsang*. At another level, I was not trying to accomplish anything at all; my attempt was just to make everyone think and re-evaluate their positions. The positions people take are a consequence of their belief system and the experiential knowledge. The mixture of belief and experiential knowledge becomes a lens, as it were, between their minds and everything else.

Everyone looks at the world, other people, and their own thoughts through this lens, which distracts, distorts, and deflects. Our entire world view, as well as self-esteem, is conditioned by this. If we want to see the world as it truly exists and see ourselves as we truly exist, we need to destroy this lens. This means that we dismantle our belief system and knowledge. The belief system is a consequence of accumulated and infused knowledge.

Essentially, we are talking of shedding all our knowledge to see the Truth, as it is, at which point, we get back to our true nature, a blissful entity. Our spiritual quest and ritual effort must be directed towards unlearning if we are to get our bliss. But invariably we set up a barter exchange in which we trade our offerings for a favour from gods. This sure moves us further away from bliss.

The 'Think Series' rolled out month after month and I continued to expand on this theme, quoting extensively from all the books I had been reading for decades. It was taking a toll on people, and slowly, steadily the participants started dropping off. It was perhaps very confusing to listen to a guy who asked them to come and *learn how to unlearn while constantly demanding that they should not listen to anyone.* I was not offering any alternative belief, idol, or an idea, but pushing a concept that *no idea really mattered.*

Frankly that did not matter to me as well. Whether their participation in my sessions helped them or not, *their non-participation helped me a lot.* Slowly, all the books I had been reading for decades made sense; Socrates, Plato, Yajnavalkya, Ashtavakra, Zarathustra, Rabbi Jesus and everyone else made sense. All the rituals and idols that I had discounted made sense.

Human minds need something to grasp before launching further—the way pole-vaulters run long and push the pole on a fulcrum position on ground before leaping high. If they learn to drop the pole, they go far; if they get stuck at the fulcrum, unwilling to let the pole go, they crash. It became clear to me that all the things I had ridiculed were helpful *only* for those who were *willing to let them go.* Those who sanctified and worshipped the books, gurus, and gods were left behind, as they clung to them. Quite paradoxical indeed.

This lens, born to ego and belief system, was creating a universe for myself, crowning me as the emperor with everything moving as I desired. But it was so flimsy that it collapsed at the very first contact with someone else's universe. Well, they had their own universe created by their own lenses. There was no way of determining which of the multitude of universes so created was the real thing; everyone believed their own thing is more real than others, which was probably true for them and only them.

The 'Think Series' had come a full circle. It actually stopped my thinking, and I was at peace. If I had thought that the conversations were coming to end, I was in for a surprise. The 'Think Series' gave way for not one but two conversations.

One was the 'Act' series, where a dozen of us decided to explore how we could actually imbibe and act on the lofty principles. This led to open-ended, 'no agenda' conversation which disproved many common notions. While the tide of life tosses people around as if they were mere dry leaves, their inner core is always steadily driven by their convictions.

We witness so much of diversity at the surface levels that we fail to see the unity at the core. So many know so much, having accomplished so much, and yet we just fail to take notice of them; on their part, they play ignorant, either because *they don't know that they actually know* or because they don't think it is needed to show.

The second offspring conversation was very interesting and a great eye-opener. We called it 'Happiness' session, not even 'quest for happiness' session. I had the honour of facilitating a conversation about happiness to a group of 'local' Americans who have not had access to Indian philosophical thought. I created a cocktail of topics mixing cognitive psychology, marketing, Abrahamic theology, and Patanjali Yoga Sutra to create a framework for achieving happiness.

The inquisitiveness, open mind, rigour, logic, and disciplined internalisation that those Americans demonstrated was truly a humbling experience. All the preconceived notions of America were so off the mark.

It was yet another reminder of the futility of the mental models we have built that cause so much of misunderstanding and misery. The sooner we unlearn many of these, the better it will be for us.

As the train chugged along, it was all falling in place in my dream. My guru was right; he had taught me everything through his silence, glances, and occasional words, and it had taken me nearly thirty years to get it. It no longer mattered who I really was or if my true nature was blissful; they were both equally irrelevant ideas.

What mattered was a realisation that I was connected as it were with every living and non-living thing in the universe. It was as if an infinite sheet of consciousness had millions of bubbles that we call our own personal identity. This guy who is now travelling in the *Acela Express* from Boston will continue to think and act in the way he designed the lens. But he now knows that he is much more than that. The more he unlearns, the more learned he would become.

The train conductor made the announcement that we were reaching Metropark station in New Jersey, my stop. He advised us to check and ensure we take our prized possessions with us, not leaving them behind.

I smiled to myself and got down with my thoughts; I picked up my rental car and drove down to our office in Bridgewater City and met the head of Americas, Mr Ashok Vemuri. He was young, bright, and very focused, carrying the burden of billions of dollars' business as if it did not matter. He walked gently and talked softly, but every syllable counted.

'This is our next battle as we try to change the way we work in America' his voice rang out as he started defining his vision.

This guy who is listening to Ashok will get ready and fight his next battle with vigour. He will win some, lose some, but will continue the journey unaltered.

EPILOGUE

The snow stopped, and there was eerie quiet out there. It seemed that ultimately the patience of us Bostonians won and the nor'easter had to beat a hasty retreat. It ran away as fast as it could into the warm waters of the Atlantic Ocean.

For us Bostonians, facing a foot of snow was commonplace, and we continued life as if nothing had happened. Snowploughs of various sizes swung into action, and within hours the snow was off the road. People started to drive around, trying to catch up with life. Whether Stop & Shoppe opens for business or not, Patel's will be there with their Seven-Elevens, ready to sell milk, bread, soda, and the lottery tickets. I put down the seventh cup of hot tea and got out of the couch.

Plenty of shovelling has to be done; the long flight of steps that led us down the hill in front of the door has to be cleared. This time around, the nor'easter dumped more snow than usual, and with the snowploughs pushing a mountain of snow on the front yard, even the fire hydrant had gotten buried. I need to wade through three feet of snow and clear a pathway to the fire hydrant. Town laws need to be obeyed in New England if you did not want to be fined.

I also have to get ready for my next battle, as outlined by Ashok, and unleash changes that Infosys had not seen yet in America. Neither of us had any idea what they might be, but both of us were sure we would prevail. We were experienced and battle-scarred enough to know that our success amongst ambiguity did not come from leveraging anything we knew already. We will have unlearn them, and learn something new on the fly as we wade through the unknown.

My battles will not stop, my travels will not stop, and my learning from life will not stop, as long as I live. If there were a way I could learn even after death, I would gladly do so.

The paradox is that I will continue to *unlearn* as commanded by my guru. Learning and unlearning will have to go hand in hand, as we exist as an individual identity as well as a universal connected entity. The individual identity is sustained by this incessant learning; without it, the identity is blurred and the purpose is lost. The universal identity, on the other hand, is incumbent on unlearning what the individual has learnt.

This was perhaps the most practical postulate made by the eighth-century philosopher Shankara in his philosophical edifice, *Advaitha Vedanta*. He split the reality into two parts, a pragmatic reality and a super reality—the former being relevant to our daily life as conditioned individuals and the latter for the *nirvana* seekers. One could easily guess that 'super reality' meant sublimation of conditioned existence that was replaced by all-pervading, intelligent, eternal, and blissful existence.

It was a brilliant psychological move that gave the much-needed space and opportunity for people to be imperfect, while on warpath to perfection.

I had to finish clearing the snow-covered path for my fellow seekers of the neighbourhood who will be trooping in for the last *satsang*, before we moved to New Jersey. The 'Happiness' guys, Peter, Paul, Heather, Robin, and Sandhya will come and say goodbye. As a parting gift I will have to give them a cheat sheet I designed for applying the *yamas* and *niyamas* of Ashtanga Yoga. Among many things, the cheat sheet will define greed that Yogi Patanjali suggested we avoid.

The 'Act' guys, Kumar, Subha, Sundar, Mohan and Jayanthi will also come in to have one more debate about what remains once we dismantle all the constructs listed in Sankhya Karika.

For those of us who have been inspired by the legendary Japanese warriors samurais, the constant dread is to avoid becoming a Ronin. We live by the Samurai codes of mastery, loyalty, honour, and wisdom. We would rather die in honour following a vision, than fail to live a Ronin, a Samurai who left his master to die unprotected. It would be a life of shame.

Our journey continues. Our learning and unlearning will so continue.

Forever.

ACKNOWLEDGEMENTS

It is always written by famous authors that it is impossible to acknowledge every one that contributed to the writing of a book. Countless people shape up our lives, and so all of them contribute to our thought process. I am no different from any other author. So here is my acknowledgement to all the people whom I have met so far in my life who have knowingly and unknowingly contributed.

There are two sets of people who I want to acknowledge specifically, those who shaped my life and those who shaped my life and this book.

Let me start with the first set of people. At the outset, I must credit my parents for giving me this life and freedom to experiment and pursue whatever I wanted in life. This can never be repaid. The role played by my brothers, sister, and their spouses cannot be rated.

My childhood and college friends who gave me all the selfless joy is acknowledged. The influence my 'glass mates', PMJay, VKJK, Naren, and Kamesh, has been immense. They, along with Jyoti and Sheila, never lost faith in me, though I continued to give disappointing performance. At every turn of frustration, I looked at them and drew comfort and courage. To this day, even after forty years, their faith in me has been undiminished, and they were truly overjoyed when I announced the publication of this book. Thank you, buddies.

My first manager, who is not named in the book, deserves special acknowledgement. Not everyone gets to be told they are unwelcome on the very first minute of their career. I had that unique experience, and he gave me that, and made me a man of tough spirits. So thank you, Mr First Manager.

The way the managing directors of GO & GE Medical System, Murali and DAP, shaped me into a good leader by challenging and personally mentoring me is noteworthy.

Words cannot express the influence India's Jack Welch, Shibulal, CEO of Infosys, had on me. I had the honour of working with him as he and Nandan grew the company to a multi-billion-dollar globally admired enterprise. I am deeply indebted to him for providing challenging opportunities that provided the battleground to successfully test many of the paradox principles that form the backbone of this book.

To say that I was inspired by 'NRN' Narayana Murthy is commonplace. Every interaction I had with him changed me forever. It was a rare and great honour to have met him one-on-one so many times. What was more impactful was he taught me how to push the teams hard without breaking them down.

There were many executives among our clients who gave me the space to experiment my paradox principles, encouraging me and even adopting my views. Scott Griffin, Gabe Hanzeli, and Heather Campbell are among the many whose interactions shaped up my principles.

As leaders, we can devise any strategy we like and any fancy principles we may want. Results validate them, and those results depend on the lieutenants we have. I was very lucky to have been blessed with extraordinarily talented lieutenants like Mihir, Ramki, Jayanth, Raghav, Sreedhar, Andrew, Tom, and Sesh. Their success is the validation of the paradox principles.

Family is the first editorial board that new authors have to deal with; they are the first copy editors who help polish the writing as well. But for my family's support, this book would not have been possible.

I must record my sincere gratitude for my wife, Jayanthi, who was the stabilising force in my life, as I moved like a tornado around the world. She is an accomplished writer, artist, interior decorator, and above all, a good, kind person. When I started developing the theme of the book, she spent hours helping me understand the art of writing. She went through my first draft and patiently explained the story-telling, ignoring my Yajnvalkya-type pride. When I now look at the very first draft in my drafts folder, I know how far I have come, thanks to her guidance.

I thank my son, Arvind, who told me that writing letters is not telling a story. That single statement helped me understand the problem of my writing style. I have sincerely tried to improve, and I hope he likes it.

My daughter, Aparna, my diamond, provided a feedback that helped me connect the dots of multiple episodes mentioned. She almost drew a process of how to do it. As usual, it was direct and addressed the crux of the issues.

My son-in-law, Dr Deepak Hegde, found time amidst his busy schedule of teaching in NYU Stern, research work, and consulting to review the draft. When he said it is tough to combine Dale Carnegie, Chandler, and R. K. Narayan, I was really stunned, as that was what I attempted. His advice on mercilessly checking the relevance of anecdotes was immensely helpful.

No amount of acknowledging will match the effort U. B. Pravin Rao put in to patiently review the whole book. As one of the leading senior executives at Infosys, he is extremely busy and still found time to do this. Pravin is a leader of the rarest breed and virtually everyone at Infosys want to work for him. Thank you, 'real' Rao!

Finally, I thank the Penguin group for encouraging first-time authors like me.

Did I forget to acknowledge myself for putting in those late-night writing hours as a busy Infosys executive? How could I do that? Thanks a ton, Paddy Rao.